Codifying New Url

How to Reform Municipal Land Development Regulations

CONGRESS FOR THE NEW URBANISM

TABLE OF CONTENTS

CHARTER OF THE NEW URBANISM

THE CONGRESS FOR THE NEW URBANISM views disinvestment in central cities, the spread of placeless sprawl, increasing separation by race and income, environmental deterioration, loss of agricultural lands and wilderness, and the erosion of society's built heritage as one interrelated community-building challenge.

WE STAND for the restoration of existing urban centers and towns within coherent metropolitan regions, the reconfiguration of sprawling suburbs into communities of real neighborhoods and diverse districts, the conservation of natural environments, and the preservation of our built legacy.

WE RECOGNIZE that physical solutions by themselves will not solve social and economic problems, but neither can economic vitality, community stability, and environmental health be sustained without a coherent and supportive physical framework.

WE ADVOCATE the restructuring of public policy and development practices to support the following principles: neighborhoods should be diverse in use and population; communities should be designed for the pedestrian and transit as well as the car; cities and towns should be shaped by physically defined and universally accessible public spaces and community institutions; urban places should be framed by architecture and landscape design that celebrate local history, climate, ecology, and building practice.

WE REPRESENT a broad-based citizenry, composed of public and private sector leaders, community activists, and multidisciplinary professionals. We are committed to reestablishing the relationship between the art of building and the making of community, through citizen-based participatory planning and design.

WE DEDICATE ourselves to reclaiming our homes, blocks, streets, parks, neighborhoods, districts, towns, cities, regions, and environment.

For the full Charter, see Appendix B.

INTRODUCTION
New Urbanism and Codes

by Jonathan Barnett, FAICP

Some years ago, when I became the director of urban design for the New York City Planning Commission, I was amazed to learn how many of the problems with the built environment in the city—problems which I had always blamed on developers and their architects—turned out to be mandated by the city's zoning and other codes. Cities had drawn up these laws for rational purposes, but the people who drew them up did not understand their physical consequences. My colleagues and I helped write some of the earliest special zoning districts in the U.S., plus provisions that today would be called form-based coding, to overcome many of these problems. In a book that I wrote describing this experience, *Urban Design as Public Policy* (Architectural Record Books, 1974), I asked a question that is still relevant today; namely, If we can get what we ask for, why can't we get what we want? This PAS Report seeks to answer that question.

The Charter of the New Urbanism defines a series of desirable changes to the built environment. Developers, public officials, and citizens who have read the Charter or attended meetings of the Congress of the New Urbanism often wish to try out some New Urbanist ideas in their own communities. Sometimes they find what they wish to do is literally against the law or, at best, that local development regulations make many of the Charter's objectives difficult to achieve. Can local development regulations be changed to create a positive vision of the future, such as is outlined in the Charter, without these regulations losing their constitutional basis, without diminishing property values, and without becoming too difficult to administer? We think the answer is yes, and that is what this report is about.

WHAT THE CHARTER PROPOSES

The Charter outlines 27 ways to improve the design and planning of cities, towns, and regions. It foresees a future where cities and towns, edge cities, and commercial corridors have strong, compact central areas with a mix of stores, work places, and residences, surrounded by neighborhoods where children can walk or bicycle to elementary schools, and residents enjoy an environment where they meet friends while walking, cycling, or doing errands in local shops. Such development should all fit into a natural environment where farms, ranches, and woodlands have been preserved from unnecessary urbanization.

The Charter begins by identifying the region as today's fundamental economic unit and cites the need to preserve the integrity of a region's natural environment and the importance of regional transportation in giving structure to land-use and development patterns. The Charter identifies the individual town or village and the neighborhood as fundamental building blocks of urbanization and says that each should be small enough for a person to walk across in 10 minutes, meaning that bigger towns and cities should be made up of a series of walkable neighborhoods. All towns, villages, or neighborhoods should include a mix of uses, and provide for different incomes and lifestyles. The Charter also says that special-purpose districts, including compact downtowns, and corridors—both along transportation lines and following natural systems—have their place in the design and planning of regions. The street is identified by the Charter as the fundamental element in planning and designing development. The Charter says that streets should connect into patterns of blocks small enough to make communities walkable and that streets should be planned to have a strong design relationship to buildings and public places. The Charter also stresses the importance of historic preservation, making buildings environmentally friendly and assimilating automobiles into development patterns without allowing them to be the sole design determinants.

THE POWER OF DEVELOPMENT REGULATIONS

There is nothing inherent in the concept of development regulation that prevents the principles of the Charter of the New Urbanism from being implemented. On the contrary, development regulations ought to be the chief means by which the principles embodied in the Charter become reality.

Local zoning and subdivision ordinances are the most important codes to change in order to implement New Urbanist principles. Zoning laws can closely define what a developer may build, or they may be effectively meaningless. All zoning regulates the kinds of activities that may be accommodated on a given piece of land, the amount of space devoted to these activities, and the ways that buildings may be placed and shaped. In other words, zoning prescribes what may be built, how much, and where on the property it may be built. If the code is restrictive in relation to market demand, it may

The street is identified by the Charter as the fundamental element in planning and designing development.

directly control what developers build if they wish to maximize profits. That was the case in New York when I worked for the city and is still true in New York, San Francisco, Boston, and in many other places with strong real estate markets and a tradition of governmental control. Other communities, however, may be just going through the motions of regulation, with codes so permissive that just about anything can be constructed—or there may be a practice of providing amendments and variances on demand.

Subdivision ordinances, of course, contain the regulations governing the division of properties into smaller lots. Standards governing the design and grading of streets, the size and shape of lots, and the allocation and placement of open space are all found there. Subdivision provisions limiting the grade of streets are often the unwitting cause of the destructive stripping and regrading of the natural environment that takes place in developing suburban and exurban areas. The street standards in subdivision regulations are frequent causes of unnecessarily wide streets and turning radii.

If codes are going to play a positive role in shaping the built environment, they need to be carefully related to the real estate market, they need to be rewritten to achieve positive outcomes as well as guarding against abuses, and they need to be consistently administered.

HOW RELEVANT ARE ZONES TODAY?

Zoning divides the landscape into zones or districts, each of which is given a specific regulatory character. Most people still believe it important to separate heavy industry from residences and to keep uses that generate a lot of traffic close to major roads, but the idea that each different land use needs to be separated from all the others and that different densities of development also need to be separated is no longer axiomatic. Most planners, developers, and communities today agree there are many occasions when a mix of uses is desirable, and many places where there can and should also be a mix of different densities.

Every zoning ordinance contains two parts: the text, which defines each zone, and the map, which shows where each zone is located. Both need to be carefully evaluated if they are to function as positive design management tools and not as impediments to the best development. The list of permitted uses articulated in the text for each zone is the means of enforcing what can often be an undesirable amount of separation. A desire to make zoning maps demonstrably objective has lead to a presumption in favor of large districts that extend over areas of similar development and against a mix of smaller districts that include only one or a few property owners (such districts are often created by "spot zoning") unless there are clear defining or preexisting circumstances to justify the smaller zones. A combination of unnecessarily exclusive zones, plus mindless mapping of these zones over big areas, is a big part of the recipe for suburban sprawl.

The text also typically contains what are called "bulk provisions" for each zone. These directly shape buildings by setting limits to the amount of floor area, the height, and such placement issues as setbacks. After World War II, there was a shift in zoning practice from reliance on bulk controls to regulate the size and shape of buildings to a new emphasis on floor area ratios (FARs) that relate the amount of development permitted to the area of the lot. The difficulty is that the FAR is really an occupancy control and generally excludes parts of buildings like mechanical floors, stairways, and elevator cores. Many codes even exclude aboveground parking garages from floor area calculations on the principle that they are not occupied spaces. Experience has shown that FARs by themselves give communities little control over the shape and placement of buildings and need to be supplemented with more traditional height, setback, and build-to standards.

Most planners, developers, and communities today agree there are many occasions when a mix of uses is desirable, and many places where there can and should also be a mix of different densities.

WHAT IS WRONG WITH ZONING AND SUBDIVISION REGULATIONS?

The biggest problem with zoning and subdivision regulations is that, while individual provisions are continually amended in attempts to bring them up to date, the original concepts were formulated in the period just after World War I, and they no longer correspond to current ideas about a desirable society, to current development patterns, or to the way that the modern real estate industry operates.

A Basic Problem with All Zoning

When zoning codes were first written, the interactions between the built and natural environments were not as well understood as they are today. Almost all zoning codes treat land as a commodity to be allocated among various uses and not as a living eco-system to be preserved as well as developed. The increasing prevalence of flooding in developed areas is just one indication of why zoning codes need to be amended to protect natural areas if the regional ecological balance is to be maintained.

Problems with Residential Zoning

Residential zones are usually written as a continuum based on density (i.e., number of families per lot, lot size, and building type). At one end of the spectrum are single-family houses on large lots and, at the other end, tall apartment houses. Each of these different house and lot types is customarily given a different zone, although before zoning most cities and towns had a variety of different house types and densities within each residential neighborhood. The assumption that residential zones should be divided along a continuum from the most-protected, single-family houses on large lots in country or estate areas to high-density apartment buildings in city centers reflects development patterns and concepts of social hierarchy that existed in the 1920s. At that time, social leaders in big cities could be found living in townhouses or luxury apartment buildings in a few elite downtown neighborhoods, but, in general, people who lived in apartments, duplexes, triplexes, or rowhouses were considered to be of lower social standing than people who lived in single-family detached houses. Families that lived in small houses on small lots, in turn, were thought to be of lower social standing than people who lived in bigger houses on bigger lots.

This hierarchy also corresponded to the organization of cities in the 1920s, where a core of downtown commercial uses and exclusive downtown neighborhoods was surrounded by a ring of manufacturing and "slum" housing. The next ring out from the downtown core was the location for the streetcar suburbs of apartments, attached houses, and smaller single-family residences. The residential suburbs for larger houses were reached by train or automobile and occupied the farthest ring out. These suburbs generally were zoned to exclude industry, and apartments were confined to a small central commercial district. Beyond this outer ring was a rural area of farms and country estates, often the summer homes of people who lived in town houses or apartments in the elite downtown residential districts.

This 1920s hierarchical city can still be discerned as an underlying element in today's far more complicated development pattern and much more open society. But today the size of a house or lot is as likely to be a lifestyle decision as a social indicator. The development industry now operates at a scale unimagined in the 1920s, while modern highways and car ownership have permitted the extension of cities and suburbs far beyond their dimensions 80 years ago. The bias in zoning administration towards mapping large, single-use districts, combined with residential zoning's original exclusionary character, has created the modern housing tracts of same-size houses on same-size lots built by corporate development organizations at a scale not anticipated when zoning codes were originally drafted. The fact that residential regulations create new subdivisions, not neighborhoods or communities, is a major problem. Some recent suburban subdivisions may consist of townhouses or garden apartments, but the problem is the same: large tracts of single-size residential units.

The Charter of the New Urbanism defines neighborhoods, not housing tracts, as the basic building blocks for cities and towns. When a developer wants to build a new neighborhood with a mix of house sizes and some apartments, and perhaps a convenience store or two, there are usually no zoning districts in the code that permit this type of development.

The problem can be overcome to some extent with special measures like planned unit development (PUD) amendments to the code or traditional neighborhood development (TND) codes. These are special procedures, however, treated as an exception to the rule rather than as a corrective to the rule. The underlying hierarchical bias in residential zoning still needs to be addressed.

The Charter of the New Urbanism defines neighborhoods, not housing tracts, as the basic building blocks for cities and towns.

Problems with Commercial Zoning

When zoning codes were originally drafted, most commercial development was expected to take place in big-city downtowns, on neighborhood commercial streets, or in small-scale downtowns in residential suburbs. The codes did not anticipate modern patterns of distributed commercial development: the suburban office park, the regional shopping mall, or the suburban commercial corridor or strip. These development types have been distorted by the preexisting zoning codes or zoning precedents.

The zoning districts that accommodated the linear Main Street in a small town or suburb, or the commercial corridor along a streetcar route in an urban neighborhood, have been extended and mapped for miles along arterial streets in cities and suburbs. This commercial strip zoning does not work at such a large scale. It is dysfunctional for traffic movement, as shoppers making turns conflict with drivers headed for more distant destinations. There is too much land mapped as commercial zones to be used efficiently and too little at the most desirable commercial locations along the corridor. These zoning districts often don't permit residential development at all, so that the logical corrective—transforming points along these overextended Main Streets into town centers with a mix of uses—is not permitted by the zoning.

Suburban office headquarters or office parks often began in estate areas that had been opened up to such development by new highways. These exclusive residential districts were in many cases remapped to exclusive commercial zones, but the resulting office parks do not have the support of other kinds of commercial uses that could supply food, hotels, and other services for office workers and business visitors. Current zoning usually does not permit office parks to evolve into a more balanced form of development.

The regional shopping mall has been built near highway interchanges, which provide a comparable level of access to a traditional downtown. But these malls are isolated from other commercial uses, such as hotels or office buildings, or the high-density residential zones that support shopping in traditional downtowns. In many places, the real-estate market would support adding apartments or townhouses to these shopping mall locations, producing the beginnings of a compact, mixed-use development that could be served by transit. Again, the obstacle is usually zoning.

Problems with Industrial Zoning

Most problems with industrial zoning concern the map and not the text. There continues to be a consensus that industrial uses that cause pollution or draw large amounts of truck traffic should be separated from commercial and residential development. The problem is that industrial districts in the central areas of older cities are no longer suitable for most modern industrial users, while they may well be suitable for adaptive use as residences, offices, or both. Meanwhile, it is difficult to locate new industrial zones because of the absence of effective regional planning. It may be that realizing the principles of the Charter of the New Urbanism in locating industry will require shifting some industrial zoning functions to the same kinds of Metropolitan Planning Organizations that serve as clearinghouses for transportation proposals.

The biggest zoning text problem for industrial uses in individual cities and towns is managing the transition away from industrial uses in older areas without forcing out jobs that are still badly needed in these communities. In many cases, a transition to a mixed-use zone is the answer. There are many uses classified as industrial that are compatible with other forms of development and could be included in compact, walkable, mixed-use business centers.

Don't Forget the Subdivision Codes

Many important New Urbanist ideas, like regulating block size, keeping streets in scale with development, making streets connect, and reserving sites for civic buildings need to be added to subdivision codes, which currently relate mostly to individual lots. Grading requirements in subdivision codes need to be restudied in light of current knowledge about conserving the natural environment.

HOW TO CHANGE THE CODES

Cities and towns have been building in accordance with zoning and subdivision for several generations. It is clear that some of the original concepts and methods are no longer appropriate and that it is time to change the codes. This will not be easy. Changing codes can affect property values for individual owners, and changing regulations means future changes to a community. Property owners are conservative, and communities have become suspicious of change precisely because so much new development has been warped by outmoded regulations into results that people don't like.

The first and most critical point is that people who believe in the principles of the Charter of the New Urbanism and understand that development regulations need to change belong to a group that is growing all the time. All across the U.S., communities have begun making such changes to their development regulations. There is more and more experience about how to do it. One of the purposes of this PAS Report is to bring together some of these experiences as well as presenting the theoretical framework needed to make comprehensive changes.

In Chapter 1, the authors outline the foundations of New Urbanist zoning, such as decreasing emphasis on uses and use-separation, putting more emphasis on building form and the planning of larger areas. They also list a series of code changes that can be implemented relatively quickly and that will go a long way towards realizing New Urbanist objectives. Chapter 2 outlines the steps towards more comprehensive regulatory reform and provides a series of code-drafting principles. Chapter 3 describes the links between New Urbanist principles and regulations with detailed descriptions of ordinances and provisions that relate to the objectives of the Charter. Paul Crawford has contributed an Afterword in which he shows that codes are only one aspect of a community's system of development management. He offers advice on how to reform the whole development management system. Appendix A includes a survey of New Urbanist development regulations already adopted. There are also sidebars distributed throughout the text

The first and most critical point is that people who believe in the principles of the Charter of the New Urbanism and understand that development regulations need to change belong to a group that is growing all the time.

including commentary from a long-time planning director and a planning consultant, both of whom are committed to the implementation of New Urbanist principles.

The authors hope that this PAS Report will prove to be a useful and effective guide for teaching, understanding, and, most importantly, implementing the principles of the Charter of the New Urbanism. As Chapters 1 and 2 make clear, the ideas and methods of New Urbanism can be incorporated into local land development regulations in a variety of ways. As Chapter 3 illustrates, New Urbanism can and has been achieved in real places, and, furthermore, many people have made it clear that they want these changes for their community.

CHAPTER 1
New Urbanist Essentials

by Joel Russell

Bridging the gap between the general principles set forth in the Charter of the New Urbanism and the details of local development regulations may appear to be a daunting task. Some approaches, however, involve only a few simple steps, while others are far more complicated. New Urbanist practitioners have developed a wide variety of approaches to regulatory reform. The following principles make it possible to use zoning and other land use regulations to achieve the interrelated goals of New Urbanism. These elements of New Urbanist zoning are followed by a discussion of more detailed regulatory provisions. Chapter 2 follows with recommendations for a process to initiate reform of local land development regulations.

Before delving into the objectives and details of New Urbanist code reform, the discussion below sets the stage by explaining what we mean by the term "code," a word that is used in many different ways by practitioners.

DIFFERENT TIERS AND KINDS OF "CODES": A CONTINUUM FROM PLANNING TO DESIGN

The word "code" creates considerable confusion because it can mean many different things in different contexts. On one level, it can be the land-use ordinance or body of land-use ordinances that govern all land development within a municipality (e.g., the San Antonio Unified Development Ordinance). This type of code or ordinance is general because it has to cover a large geographic area. It provides the overall framework and set of rules within which individual projects are designed and approved. At the opposite end of the spectrum, a code can be a set of very specific design instructions for a specific project or even a specific building within a project (e.g., the design code for Seaside, Florida). This type of code often establishes parameters for the architecture of individual buildings to ensure that each contributes to the creation of the urban character of the whole development. In between, there are codes that govern large multi-faceted projects, groups of related projects, or specific areas within a municipality, such as the Regulating Plan for the Central Waterfront of Hercules, California.

I'On was approved by Town of Mount Pleasant South Carolina through a planned development ordinance with design regulated by The I'On Code, prepared by the developer. The Code was adopted by the Town and attached to and made part of the ordinance that approved the project. The emphasis of the code was on creating a traditional walking neighborhood built in the manner of older South Carolina coastal towns.

Brian Bowman

New Urbanist practice is distinguished by its emphasis on detailed design codes for individual neighborhoods, streets, and buildings (and the "projects" that encompass these). It is difficult to achieve the kind of fine-grained detailing of the public realm at the heart of the New Urbanism without specifying how this is to be done at the site-specific level. Most of the discussion of codes and coding among New Urbanists is focused on this level of detail. In fact, early New Urbanist projects were largely produced by designers and developers working to create a type of urbanism at odds with the local zoning regulations. The experience of these early New Urbanist practitioners in doggedly pursuing rezonings and planned unit development (PUD) approvals led to the recognition of the need for broader regulatory provisions to implement New Urbanism.

The importance of detailed site-specific design codes, in many ways at the heart of New Urbanist practice, cannot be overstated. Without a revolution in the way codes are written for larger geographic areas, however, New Urbanism might remain scattered islands of urbanity surrounded by a sea of suburban sprawl.

In thinking about the different types of codes described in the following sections, keep in mind the important variables in each.

Public vs. Private vs. "Joint"

Codes governing an entire municipality (town, city, county) are always "public": they are adopted as laws by local governing bodies. A municipal zoning ordinance is an example of a public code. On the other hand, a code consisting of design covenants imposed by a developer and administered by the developer and/or a property owners association is "private": there is no governmental entity involved in approving or administering it. The design code for Seaside, Florida, is an entirely private code (it is actually a series of codes for homeowners associations on each street). Many developments that are approved through a PUD process, traditional neighborhood development (TND) provision, or Specific Plan contain detailed design standards drafted by a developer but ultimately incorporated into the municipality's formal approval of the project. These are "joint" codes: they are drafted by the developer and approved by the municipality. Depending on the circumstances, they may be administered and enforced privately, publicly, or both. The codes discussed in this PAS Report are all public codes, some of which were developed jointly by public and private entities.

Tiers

It is useful to think in terms of tiers of planning and design regulation. At the level of the region, there are no codes at all in the American context, and very few plans. Within a municipality, there is usually a set of land-use regulations adopted by local government. These may provide for local area or project-specific planning and regulation, such as the Master Plan for a PUD or a Regulating Plan for a TND. When these codes are administered entirely privately, they are private codes as described above. When incorporated into municipal approvals or adopted as a Specific Plan, they become the public land-use law for the regulated area. The approval processes specific to these project areas typically nest within the framework of the municipal ordinance, providing for progressively more detailed regulation as the project area gets smaller.

Size of Area Covered—Planning vs. Design

Codes that cover very large areas are more likely to be public and general, with an emphasis on planning procedures and general standards. These procedures and standards may, in turn, create a mechanism for planning and designing at the project level with more specific and design-oriented content. There may be an intermediate tier, which is an area containing multiple projects subject to the same set of land-use rules, as in the Southeast Sector Plan in Orlando, Florida. (See the case study in Chapter 3.)

As the area being planned becomes smaller, the code is more likely to focus on design issues. It will typically specify a site plan for streets, buildings, and buildings, and landscape features, as well as prescribe architectural and landscaping standards. Design-oriented codes usually focus more on content and less on procedures, especially where procedures are already established by the land development ordinance within which the codes nest.

Land Ownership

A code for an entire municipality must take into account the large number of landowners affected by it. As the regulated area becomes smaller (i.e., district or project scale), it may still involve multiple landowners, but it will

It is useful to think in terms of tiers of planning and design regulation.

govern an area, such as a neighborhood, planning area, district, or project, that has a unifying characteristic. When there are multiple landowners in the area, it is usually necessary to have some type of public code so that all are subject to the same set of rules and no one owner controls the others. When a code applies to a project in single ownership (e.g., by an individual or a group of landowners working in concert), it can be entirely private or can be privately prepared and approved by a public regulatory body.

Summary

The character and configuration of any given code depends upon the variables discussed above. To summarize, it will be strongly influenced by:

- the size of the area it covers;
- the extent to which it deals with site-specific design;
- whether it is adopted and/or implemented publicly or privately (or both);
- whether it covers multiple land ownerships; and
- what land-use regulations and mechanisms a local government can use as prescribed by state law.

These variables actually provide considerable room for creativity in devising the best solution for a specific situation. This variety in the use of the word "code" does not alter the basic elements of New Urbanist regulation described below, although it does result in different levels of detail and emphasis.

ELEMENTS OF NEW URBANIST ZONING

Use regulation has been the primary organizing principle in most ordinances and in many debates about development projects. As noted in Jonathan Barnett's introduction, the segregation of land uses in conventional zoning codes was based on the expectation of conflicts between uses. This emphasis on use regulation resulted in a loss of attention to the details of building design and the relationships between buildings and the street. To redress this imbalance, New Urbanist codes reduce the emphasis on use regulation, greatly simplifying use lists, while increasing the emphasis on building type, form, and design.

New Urbanists use dimensional standards differently from the way they are used in conventional zoning ordinances. As in conventional zoning, dimensional requirements control size, bulk, location, and scale, but New Urbanists use these dimensional standards more to shape the spaces between buildings than to separate them from one other. New Urbanist design standards control how buildings relate to each other, to streets, and to other public spaces. Their focus is on creating a comfortable and uplifting public realm, and they vary greatly in the extent to which they regulate architecture. Use, development, and design standards are sometimes integrated into regulations governing types of buildings, as in the Huntersville, North Carolina, and Hercules, California, examples in Chapter 3. These communities have New Urbanist regulations that, in comparison to conventional zoning, provide more flexibility in relation to uses while being more prescriptive about urban design.

Successful urbanism requires a critical mass of activity created in part through proximity of different activities. Density is necessary to place buildings close together enough to create "street walls" that shape public streetscapes. Enough people must live in a place to support the lively mix of uses essential to New Urbanist development. Equally important is the provision of a variety of housing types consistent with both urban quality and the creation of mixed-income neighborhoods. Accessory units, housing

Buildings placed at the front property line create a street wall at the mixed-use Addison Circle in Addison, Texas. The town created a new zoning district calling for the urban character subsequently realized in the project.

RTKL Associates, Inc.

over storefronts, and townhouses join single-family houses in the New Urbanist "kit of parts." The dimensional standards in New Urbanist land-use regulations allow a mix of these varied types that responds to the level of urbanism (i.e., lower overall densities in neighborhoods and higher densities in city centers) and generally discourages the type of low-density, single-use, single-dwelling-type residential development found in conventional zoning ordinances.

Make neighborhoods the building blocks of your code. New Urbanism focuses on the creation and sustenance of walkable neighborhoods. This emphasis on walkability should inform many parts of the ordinance, from mixed-use zones to residential densities to standards for maximum block size, street width, and street connectivity. Ordinances may establish maximum walking distances from homes to local services or specify the proportion of new development areas to be devoted to various neighborhood components. The Southeast Orlando Sector Plan, described in Chapter 3, provides that "each neighborhood will have a 'neighborhood center' that provides gathering places for people and walkable destinations for neighborhood-focused retail and/or civic activities" with moderate-density housing surrounding the core commercial area. Larger mixed-use centers may be supported by multiple neighborhoods.

Adopt New Urbanist standards for large-scale development of greenfields and major redevelopment sites. Many localities have well-established PUD procedures originally established to provide design flexibility, which are frequently used for major greenfield and redevelopment projects. While proponents of major projects should be allowed design flexibility, they should also be required to work within a set of standards clearly requiring essential New Urbanist features, such as minimum residential densities, interconnected streets, and a mix of uses. The flexibility historically provided to developers through the PUD process leaves too much to chance. TND ordinances that establish clear and well-defined standards to provide a regulatory option for interested developers are one common mechanism for fostering such projects. The Columbus, Ohio, TND Code described in Chapter 3 provides an example of this approach. New Urbanist neighborhoods have also been created under conventional PUD ordinances, though this approach depends upon the developer's commitment to New Urbanism and is therefore riskier for the community, as discussed in Chapter 2.

In communities with a high density of bus transit or with rail transit (existing or planned), adopt and map special standards for Transit-oriented development (TOD). TOD capitalizes on proximity to transit by creating nodes of higher intensity uses around transit stations, limiting auto-oriented uses, and ensuring good connectivity to stations. The hallmarks of effective zoning for TOD are provisions that create walkability in combination with higher residential and commercial densities and a fine-grained integration of transit stops and stations with a variety of uses. Seattle's Station Area Planning Program is a major effort to create zoning specifically for transit-oriented development, highlighted in Chapter 3.

Require essential design elements by adopting prescriptive rather than permissive provisions. Conventional ordinances fail to establish well-designed places in part because they do not codify a specific vision for the design of the community. The results are often inconsistent and unsatisfying. For example, typical dimensional requirements establish a minimum setback. As long as the building is further back than the setback line, it can be anywhere on the lot. This approach fails to create coherent street space. The New Urbanist alternative is to establish build-to lines or zones, along or within which a specified portion of the building front must be built. The

The flexibility historically provided to developers through the PUD process leaves too much to chance.

outcome is a consistent street frontage in which private buildings shape the public space of the sidewalk and street. Another example is the requirement of minimum densities for properties fronting specified types of streets.

Incorporate New Urbanist provisions into all parts of the municipal code that affect planning, design, and development. Development form is strongly influenced by subdivision regulations as well as zoning. Standards for streets and blocks—critical components of New Urbanism—may be contained in subdivision ordinances or other sections of the municipal code, and frequently require amendment to support New Urbanism. Street standards are often maintained and administered by public works departments while the buildings on a given street are regulated through the planning or community development department. One way to integrate many provisions related to New Urbanism is through a Unified Development Ordinance, such as the one in San Antonio, Texas, which is described in Chapter 3. The most common approach is to amend each code separately because this is legally more convenient and politically less controversial. Site-specific Regulating Plans or Specific Plans that integrate subdivision and zoning regulations for both private property and the public realm offer another approach to transcending the conventional separation of the various urban elements that should be addressed together.

In addition to changes to development regulations, other municipal procedures and standards should be examined and, often, changed to support implementation of New Urbanism. These may include fee schedules, capital improvement programs (CIPs), and building codes. Multiple city departments often are involved in a comprehensive effort, with community development and public works generally leading the way.

WOODFORD COUNTY: *DESIGN FOR TOMORROW*

BUILDING PLACEMENT STANDARDS

WORKPLACE BUILDINGS
ILLUSTRATIONS AND STATEMENT OF INTENT

Note: these are provided as illustrations of intent. The illustrations and statements on this page are advisory only and do not have the power of law. Refer to the STANDARD *at right for the specific prescriptions and restrictions of this* BUILDING PLACEMENT STANDARD.

Geoffrey Ferrell Associates

The *Workplace* type provides for light industrial and artisanal production and related uses in an urban form. The STREET fronted by *Workplace* buildings is a civilized space faced with office doors and windows. Buildings are set around the PERIMETER of the block with their loading bays, truck docks, and other intense activities located at the rear and away from the major STREETS. The block interior is a large, working courtyard.

DO YOUR HOMEWORK!

Study your local ordinance. Whenever zoning is amended, staff and policy makers must take into consideration the entire zoning law and body of land use regulations. This is necessary to avoid inconsistencies between sections. Deleting outmoded material may be just as important as adding new language. Before undertaking regulatory amendments, the entire regulatory framework and all applicable enabling legislation must be understood so that interventions are made in a legally correct and practically effective way.

Understand your state's enabling legislation. New Urbanist land development regulations, like other land-use controls, must find support in each state's enabling legislation. For further information, see "Enabling Legislation for Traditional Neighborhood Development" by Robert Sitkowski, Anna M. Brienich, and Brian Olm in the October 2001 issue of *Land Use Law and Zoning Digest.*

Integrate standards for streets, blocks, and buildings. A basic idea of urbanism is that streets are unified public spaces with compatible buildings facing one another across them. One way to reinforce this notion is to organize regulations by street types. A typology of street types, each of which might be accompanied by a unique set of use, dimensional, and design standards, might include: boulevards, main street and squares, secondary downtown streets, residential streets, lanes, and alleys. The Regulating Plan for Central Hercules highlighted in Chapter 3 illustrates this approach. Alternately, regulations for both streets and buildings may be organized and presented together, as in the Huntersville and Columbus regulations.

Use graphics. Design-oriented codes lend themselves to illustrations. Drawings can often communicate much more clearly than words what is permitted under or sought by the regulations and can allow the ordinance's text to be abbreviated. Inserting illustrations within the code can be very helpful. The code must make clear, however, the intent of the graphics; for instance, whether they have the weight of regulation or are merely illustrative. A related technique, pioneered by New Urbanist design professionals, is the use of graphic techniques in organizing the code itself (e.g., using a tabular rather than a traditional text format for presentation of the code). The model SmartCode (Duany Plater-Zyberk & Company 2003) is an example of a highly illustrated code.

Create procedural incentives that make New Urbanist development more advantageous than conventional development. If New Urbanist provisions are offered as an optional alternative to development under conventional standards, advantages must be provided to the developer who chooses this approach. Since time is money for a developer, putting New Urbanist development on a faster approval track is a powerful incentive. For small-scale projects in communities with planning staff, New Urbanist development standards should be clear enough to be administered by staff without requiring discretionary board approvals. For large-scale projects, discretionary reviews are more likely to be required, but they should be consolidated to the extent legally allowable and contain clear criteria to guide decision making.

The code must make clear, however, the intent of the graphics; for instance, whether they have the weight of regulation or are merely illustrative.

ESSENTIAL REGULATORY PROVISIONS FOR IMPLEMENTING NEW URBANISM

In this section, seven regulatory objectives are used to synthesize the 27 principles of the Charter of the New Urbanism while keeping the big picture in view. Each of the seven is followed by detailed advice on regulatory actions (i.e., specific provisions that are the hallmarks of New Urbanist regulation).

While only some ordinances will incorporate every one of the provisions suggested here, most should be incorporated into all ordinances intended to implement New Urbanist principles.

Many community leaders want to know what they can do immediately to make their land-use regulations implement New Urbanism. By translating key principles into specific regulatory changes, a community can start to change its development pattern without having to completely overhaul its code. Chapter 2 describes how a local approach can start with strategic changes and then proceed to comprehensive regulatory reform. If the community is committed, some fundamental changes are easy to do, and some can be done in isolation from large-scale changes requiring more time.

> ### OBJECTIVE 1:
> ### Allow a variety of uses in order to create vitality and bring many activities of daily living within walking distance of homes.

The signature characteristic of Euclidean zoning—widely used throughout the country—is the separation of uses and their dispersion through minimum lot-size requirements. New Urbanists reverse this approach to bring many activities into proximity, in the interest of convenience, walkability, and liveliness. Emphasizing mixed use does not mean eliminating blocks that consist of housing only. Mixed-use neighborhoods traditionally include residential blocks with a variety of densities and housing types within a neighborhood distinguished by many activities within comfortable walking distance of most homes (Figure 1).

Complementary uses set within an interconnected street network bring together essential aspects of community life and minimize reliance on the car. A compact, mixed-use pattern (below)— fundamental to New Urbanism— contrasts with the Euclidian separation (above) that characterizes conventional suburban development.

FIGURE 1. EUCLIDEAN SEPARATION VS. MIXED-USE INTEGRATION

EUCLIDEAN SEPARATION

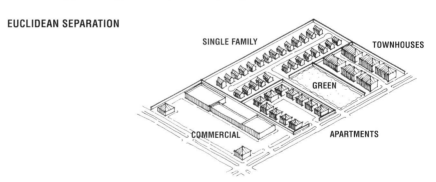

MIXED-USE INTEGRATION

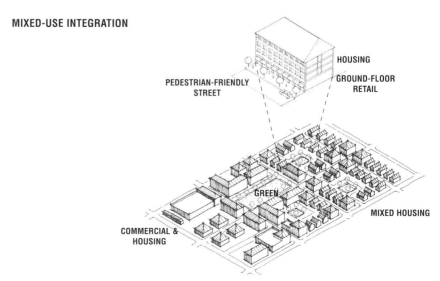

FOSTERING A VARIETY OF USES

Create mixed-use districts. Create mixed-use zoning districts that allow by-right, a fine-grained combination of uses, especially within downtown core areas, suburban activity centers, and neighborhood centers of varying scales. The Southeast Orlando Sector Plan described in Chapter 3 lays out the different uses that would best fit in centers of various scales.

Create mixed-use neighborhoods. Create neighborhood districts that allow corner stores, civic uses, and a mix of housing types in predominantly residential areas within walking distance of mixed-use centers or Main Streets.

Increase and regulate density. Create high-density districts that will generate a critical mass of activity and help support a mix of uses at the core. Some conventional ways of measuring residential density by dwelling units per acre are problematic because there are no incentives to build smaller units and because mixed-use buildings aren't properly addressed. A better approach, used in some conventional ordinances as well as New Urbanist ones, is regulating density by a combination of limits on total buildout expressed through maximum lot coverage, height, and other dimensional requirements. As long as those basic parameters and building type and other design requirements are met, the use mix and housing unit type can vary (unless ground-floor uses are specified as discussed below).

Make it possible to walk to parks, shops, and schools. Require that a specified percentage of new housing units be within walking distance of public schools and parks and neighborhood retail. For infill projects, allow this proximity requirement to be satisfied by providing such destination uses either within a new project or in an established neighborhood nearby.

Require ground-floor retail. Stimulate active ground-floor uses that generate pedestrian traffic, such as retail, restaurants, and personal service businesses. Where market conditions and local support are strong, ground-floor retail can be required. Where conditions are not ripe for mandated retail, require buildings that can house successful ground-floor retail by regulating fenestration, entries, and other features, while allowing offices and other nonretail uses in the short term. Over time, track market changes and adjust regulations accordingly.

Permit a mix of uses on upper floors. Permit upper floors of mixed-use buildings to contain a mix of dwelling units, offices, and miscellaneous compatible nonresidential uses (e.g., artist and artisan studios, dance studios, gyms) that generate activity during most hours of the day in the neighborhood.

Allow a variety of permitted uses. In all districts, introduce a diversity of compatible uses by right.

OBJECTIVE 2:
Foster mixed residential density and housing types.

For more than 50 years, residential development in the United States has been characterized by uniformity—of type, design, and density. Now, New Urbanist projects are recapturing a traditional form that mixes density and housing type within each block and neighborhood to allow households with different needs to live close together in the same neighborhood.

MIXING RESIDENTIAL DENSITY AND HOUSING TYPES

Mix housing types. Allow as of right or require a mix of housing types and lot sizes within neighborhoods, emphasizing in zoning regulations harmonious design and building type. Some communities specify minimum densities in certain areas to allow a range of building types and ensure that a critical mass will be created (Figures 2 and 3).

FIGURE 2. SHOP HOUSES

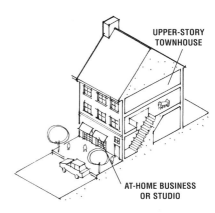

UPPER-STORY TOWNHOUSE

AT-HOME BUSINESS OR STUDIO

"Shop houses" or "live-work" townhouses combine upper-story living space with a flexible ground-floor space that can be used as a shop, art studio, or office. The combination offers an important housing alternative while adding vitality to the street and providing flexibility to accommodate different economic uses over time.

Variation in lot size and housing types helps to maintain a healthy range of household types and avoids the look of "cookie cutter" subdivisions.

FIGURE 3. MIXED DENSITY AND LOT SIZE

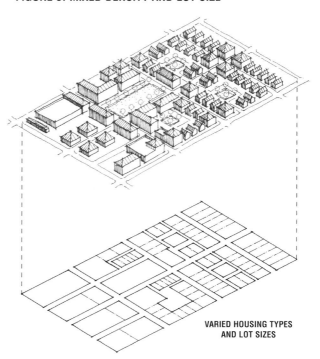

VARIED HOUSING TYPES
AND LOT SIZES

Allow accessory dwellings. Allow accessory dwellings as of right in all residential and mixed-use districts within residences as well as within detached garages and other accessory structures. For purposes of calculating density, accessory units can be exempted entirely or counted as at most one-half of a unit, reflecting their smaller impact on services than the primary dwelling. Exempting accessory units from density calculations provides maximum incentive for their construction (Figure 4).

Accessory dwellings diversify housing opportunities and provide flexibility for household needs that evolve over time. Accessory dwellings rarely need to exceed the footprint of a three-car garage (about 600 square feet). Entrances for accessory dwellings should be visible from a street or alley.

FIGURE 4. ACCESSORY DWELLINGS

SIDE DRIVE ACCESS

ALLEY-FED ACCESS

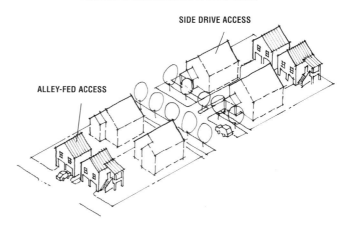

FIGURE 5. INFILL

BEFORE

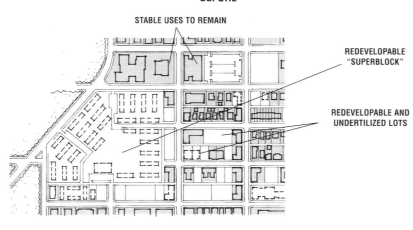

STABLE USES TO REMAIN

REDEVELOPABLE "SUPERBLOCK"

REDEVELOPABLE AND UNDERTILIZED LOTS

AFTER

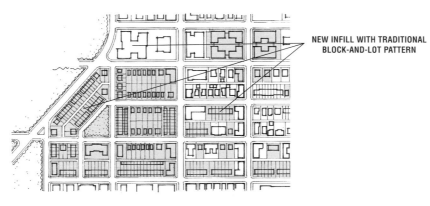

NEW INFILL WITH TRADITIONAL BLOCK-AND-LOT PATTERN

Established neighborhoods benefit when vacant and underused parcels are replaced by development that brings positive activity and "eyes on the street." Subdivision of large lots can allow a traditional block and lot pattern to be established, with new buildings fronting directly on the street and a renewed focus on the public realm.

OBJECTIVE 3:
Stimulate Infill and Rehabilitation Activity

Development of vacant and underused sites and repair and renovation of older structures strengthens existing urban areas. This is accomplished through innovative approaches to building codes as well as zoning regulations.

STIMULATING INFILL AND REHABILITATION ACTIVITY

Adjust minimum lot-size and setback requirements to reflect the smallest practical lots in the neighborhood. Increase allowable densities in infill locations to promote economically viable projects that will add vitality to the neighborhood. This may require relief from parking requirements in order to avoid the need for variances.

Expedite development review. Streamline review and permitting procedures for infill projects below a specified size threshold for projects in compliance with New Urbanist design standards. Delegate review to staff where legally permissible.

Change parking requirements. Reduce or eliminate on-site parking requirements for small-lot infill projects, allowing parking demand to be fully or partially satisfied by on-street, shared, or remote parking (Figure 6).

Revise building codes. Revise building codes to remove provisions that require rehabilitation of older buildings to current standards except when

FIGURE 6. ON-SITE PARKING

GARAGE-FREE FRONT YIELDS ADDITIONAL LANDSCAPING AND PEDESTRIAN COMFORT

CURB CUT DISPLACES ON-STREET PARKING

REQUIRED GARAGE ADDS CONSTRUCTION COSTS

On-site parking requirements add significant construction costs, which pose a problem for the developers of small infill projects. When placed in front, on-site parking also makes streets less livable. Curb cuts displace on-street parking, and driveways remove landscaping and windows from the pedestrian environment.

The Seven Fountains in West Hollywood, California, is one of a number of Southern California projects designed by Pasadena-based architects and urbanists Moule & Polyzoides, and inspired by the 1920's courtyard housing of the region.

FIGURE 7. HEIGHT TO WIDTH RATIO

APPROPRIATE FOR URBAN CONTEXT

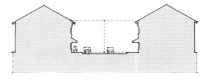

INAPPROPRIATE FOR URBAN CONTEXT

In the urban context, streets are enhanced when buildings establish a strong sense of spatial enclosure, both vertically and horizontally.

those provisions are essential for health and safety. In many states this action must be taken at the state level. (See the description of New Jersey Rehabilitation Code in Chapter 3.)

> ### OBJECTIVE 4:
> ### Develop contextual design standards that ensure that new development responds to the traditional architectural styles of the city or region.

Because private buildings shape public streets and civic spaces that together create the public realm, their design and placement are important elements of development regulations. While architectural style need not be prescribed, the Charter principles assert "architecture and landscape design should grow from local climate, topography, history, and building practice," thus avoiding the monotony of conventional suburban development and creating places of character and distinction. Regulations should be responsive to context at two levels: site-specific and regional.

FOSTERING CONTEXTUAL DESIGN

Adopt illustrated design standards. Adopt illustrated standards for building design and site design to ensure design sensitive to the regional context as well as to the site's features and immediate surroundings. Address building type and basic architectural elements rather than mandating specific styles or detail. Regulation of entries and fenestration is essential for safe and inviting streets. The streetscape can be further enhanced by addressing proportions, roof types and pitches, and materials.

Review setback and height regulations. Review and amend setback and height requirements to maintain or create ratios between the height of buildings and the distance between their facades. An appropriate relationship between the width of the streetscape and the height of buildings creates a comfortable sense of enclosure, making the public street feel like an "outdoor room." Spatial enclosure created by height-to-width ratio in urban spaces with a strong sense of place generally ranges from 1:1 to 3:1 (Figure 7).

> ### OBJECTIVE 5:
> ### Create compact, walkable centers and neighborhoods served by public transit.

A critical mass of population as well as a mix of housing types and land uses is essential to achieving the intensity of development needed to support walkable centers and to enable public transit to operate successfully.

Promote transit-supportive densities. Permit densities and concentrations of development that will support provision of transit service consistent with local and regional plans. Require minimum residential densities and lot coverage standards along existing or planned transit corridors. To support transit-oriented development, prohibit or limit auto-related uses and surface parking within transit station areas, and codify standards for pedestrian facilities that provide multiple connections to transit.

Improve parking regulations downtown. Institute parking regulations that support compact, walkable downtowns with the following provisions:

- Reduce or eliminate minimum on-site parking requirements in locations planned for highest pedestrian activity.

- Allow parking requirements to be satisfied by the use of on-street, municipal, common, or shared parking.

- Establish parking caps that limit the maximum number or total square footage of on-site surface parking spaces.

- Encourage the creation of municipal parking lots and garages by allowing payment of a fee in lieu of providing on-site parking and by encouraging landowners to dedicate rear portions of their lots for public parking.

- Prohibit off-street parking in front of buildings.

- Provide access to parking areas through alleys and side streets whenever possible.

- Make parking areas as pedestrian-friendly as possible through the use of pedestrian pathways, trees, walkways, and attractive lighting on pedestrian-scale fixtures.

- Where economically feasible, encourage the construction of multilevel parking garages that have ground-floor retails uses, are hidden in the middle of a block, or are underground.

Wide sidewalks and ground-floor shops and restaurants combine to create a lively street scene and a walkable urban district at The Corner at Eastern Market in Washington, D.C. A variance was required to allow the corner building to be built at a floor area ratio of 3.0.

Streamline development review in transit-oriented areas. Establish a by-right process facilitating construction and rehabilitation of buildings that contribute to the density, mix of uses, and urban quality essential in a transit-supportive area.

Set maximum block lengths. Establish maximum block lengths reflective of traditional patterns (generally no greater than 300 to 500 feet) to encourage pedestrian activity, to create connectivity of streets, and to provide variety in the pedestrian experience. Smaller block lengths are particularly critical in mixed-use areas.

Require street connectivity. Require streets to connect except where topography or other physical barriers make this impossible. Where streets cannot connect, require pedestrian walkways and stairways for pedestrian connectivity. A connectivity ratio can quantify this requirement while allowing for limited exceptions. The index is calculated by dividing the number of street sections between intersections, including cul-de-sacs, by the number of street nodes. For a detailed discussion of various approaches to addressing connectivity through development regulations see PAS Report No. 515, *Street Connectivity*, by Susan Handy et al.

Review street and sidewalk standards. Include standards that create an attractive environment for pedestrians. Narrower streets, with parallel on-street parking tend to reduce the speed of vehicles and enhance the sense of security of pedestrians, while shortening the crossing distance between the two sidewalks. Wider sidewalks, designed with care (e.g., sidewalks that are shaded in warm climates, offer some protection from rain, are lit well, and are furnished with benches and other conveniences) encourage pedestrian activity.

OBJECTIVE 6:
Enhance streetscapes and civic life.

In contrast to conventional zoning, New Urbanist regulations include detailed provisions for streets and civic spaces, recognizing their importance in community life and place making.

ENHANCING STREETSCAPES AND CIVIC LIFE

Make streets public spaces. Establish dimensional regulations for buildings and streets to effectively shape the streets as a public space.

Reduce or eliminate minimum setbacks. Rather than employing setbacks, use "build-to lines" or "build-to zones" (consisting of minimum and maximum setbacks). Exceptions can be allowed for civic buildings, pedestrian plazas, or outdoor eating areas in front of restaurants, cafes, or other buildings (Figure 8).

Review and amend setback and height requirements. Setback and height requirements should create desired relationships between the height of buildings and the distance between their façades as they face each other across a street (this relationship is the "enclosure ratio" described above).

Illustrate relationships between street and building elements. Street cross-sections can be used to clearly show desired building frontages, build-to lines, sidewalks, planting strips, and travelway elements.

Establish minimum lot frontage buildout requirements. Specify a minimum percentage of lot frontage to be built out with a façade at the build-to line or in the build-to zone. This type of dimensional standard helps to maintain the continuity of the street wall, an essential element (in addition to width-height ratios) of creating the feeling of an "outdoor room." Even in lower-density neighborhoods, this requirement can foster a sense of enclosure of the street.

THE MISSING LINK? REGIONAL PLANNING AND LOCAL DEVELOPMENT REGULATION

By Gianni Longo

In an ideal world, a regional plan would be the link between state planning goals (or in their absence, statewide initiatives that support Smart Growth) and the general plans that guide local governments' land-use policies. The alignment of state intentions and local government decisions through a regional plan should create a fertile environment for the harmonious growth of regions and of municipalities within them.

In the real world, however, planning and land-use decisions in a region are made by a complex web of jurisdictions and empowered bodies (counties, municipalities, townships, boards, metropolitan planning organizations, councils of governments) and are hardly ever coordinated. Among the consequences of such a fragmented decision-making environment are: sprawl; inconsistent development regulations; land-use decisions disconnected from transportation decisions; anomalous concentration of poverty in older neighborhoods and suburbs; and a disconnect between where jobs are located and where the workforce lives. These patterns of development add to congestion, environmental problems and, in general, to a deteriorating quality of life. Regional plans can bring coherence to metropolitan regions (large and small), and create a more coordinated policy framework for regulation and decision making at the local level.

In the absence of a regional form of government, local governments have the lion's share of the implementation responsibility for a regional plan. Ensuring that the recommendations of a regional plan are adopted at the local level and that they find their way first into comprehensive plans and eventually into land development codes requires strong support from elected and appointed officials. Such buy-in requires early involvement of those officials in the plan development, the identification of clear regional choices and trade offs, and the strong (and defensible) support of residents and stakeholders.

Most regional plans rely on extensive public involvement and consensus-building techniques to gain residents' and stakeholders' support. Through charrettes and vision processes, residents have an opportunity to make vital and informed decisions about the future of a region. Those decisions, if strongly supported, are difficult to ignore and can dramatically affect decision making at the local level. They can help translate a regional policy framework into locally adopted plans and land development regulations.

Put public buildings in central locations. Encourage the location of civic buildings, such as a town hall, post office, library, school, or house of worship, in visually prominent central locations. Provide design flexibility for civic buildings to allow them to make unique contributions to their surroundings.

Build neighborhood parks. Encourage small parks or squares (as small as 0.25 acre) in neighborhoods.

OBJECTIVE 7:
Shape metropolitan regions with public space, farmland, and natural areas.

The Charter of the New Urbanism places particular emphasis on the relationship between the metropolis and its agrarian surroundings and natural landscape. Local development regulations must address the potential conflict between urbanism and environmental preservation while supporting productive agriculture, rural communities, and a clear urban/rural edge. This is particularly challenging because the enactment of provisions addressing the relationship between urban and rural areas requires significant cooperation and consistent actions by neighboring localities.

SHAPING METROPOLITAN REGIONS

Define and zone the expanding metropolitan edge. The metropolitan edge—whether that of a city or a small town—needs to be defined as a distinct transitional zone, in which new development, if desired, will be carefully phased in tandem with municipal utilities, such as central sewer and water service. Use urban growth boundaries and/or annexation agreements to manage this process among neighboring urban and rural jurisdictions. Use design standards to ensure that the urban expansion area respects and echoes the character of the existing town or neighborhood.

Define and protect the most productive farmland through exclusive agricultural zoning. Where legally permissible, exclusive agricultural zoning or programs for purchase or transfer of development rights (PDRs or TDRs) will help protect productive farmland. Such zoning should allow farmers to engage in a variety of compatible small-scale businesses on their farms to enable them to supplement their farm income, especially in the off-season.

Use conservation subdivision techniques to separate and integrate open space and residential development. In areas where residential uses and active farming can co-exist, use conservation subdivision techniques to establish defined neighborhoods surrounded by protected open space or farmland. Because residential development in close proximity to intensive agriculture often produces conflict over noise, dust, and odors, such developments must be carefully designed to buffer farms from their residential neighbors.

FIGURE 8. THE BUILD-TO LINE

COMPATIBLE STREET FRONTAGE

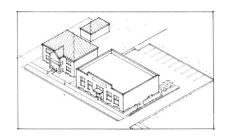

INCOMPATIBLE STREET FRONTAGE

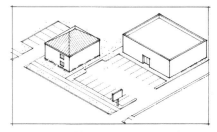

Bringing buildings, entrances, and windows to the street adds to street activity, surveillance, and a sense of spatial enclosure. Codes should include "build-to," "build-near-to," or maximum setback requirements to attain this goal.

CHAPTER 2
Putting New Urbanism to Work in Your Community

by Joel Russell

Chapter 1 uncovers the DNA of New Urbanist zoning—the critically important instructions that, when incorporated into regulatory provisions, can preserve traditional urbanism, change a mature place for the better, or give a new place the right start. This chapter addresses the practical questions of how to insert that DNA into your local land development regulations.

The principles of New Urbanism effectively demand that regulatory reform address the whole municipality—and even beyond—by creating a link to the region's form. Unfortunately, the goal of comprehensive implementation is not immediately attainable in many cases because of the practical and political difficulties of working at all scales simultaneously. Undertaking New Urbanist regulatory reform therefore requires a deliberate process of determining scale, sequence, and strategy. This process, like any successful community planning endeavor, will benefit from the participation of a wide range of members of the public as well as the involvement of members of the planning commission and local legislative body. A community education process about the principles and techniques of New Urbanism may also be needed to built support for and understanding of zoning reform.

AN INTERVIEW WITH
RICHARD BERNHARDT

Executive Director of the
Planning Commission of
Nashville-Davidson County, Tennessee

Editor's Note: An interview with Richard Bernhardt, FAICP, appears in the margins of this report throughout this chapter. Steve Bodzin conducted the interview in March 2003. It relates Bernhardt's experience in becoming a New Urbanist planner and advocate.

Tell me a bit about who you are.

I have a Masters degree in Planning, and I've been a planning director for about 25 years. Initially I was in a small combined city and county near Nashville, Tennessee, then in Gainesville, Florida, for three years, then in Orlando, Florida, for 17 years, and now in Nashville for the last three years. Over the past few years, I've been getting more involved in the improvement and writing of codes.

**How did you become a
New Urbanist planner?**

Back in the 1970s, I realized that planners needed to be more proactive. We needed a specific vision or goal. That required different tools. In the early 1980s in Orlando, I realized that there was a different pattern in the older part of town. The codes were not made to deal with an urban pattern.

From 1981 to 1983, Orlando adopted a new tier for urban areas. It was more like the 1926 code in that city, with build-to lines and other ideas that had disappeared in the modern code. It was more form-based. We worked with Andres Duany on one and developed one of the first drafts of the SmartCode into a parallel code. We made project-specific and area-specific codes to encourage New Urbanism.

In Nashville, the code adopted in 1999 is not beneficial to neighborhoods. We've been making an alternative code for the urban area, and a parallel code with conservation subdivisions and traditional neighborhoods for the greenfield areas.

This chapter begins by describing four basic steps to New Urbanist regulatory reform:

(1) Diagnosis
(2) Determining whether interim regulations are needed
(3) Selecting an approach
(4) Drafting new regulations

It goes on to address some of the tricky questions facing planners and decision makers responsible for implementing New Urbanism in their own communities.

STEPS TO REGULATORY REFORM

STEP 1:
Diagnosis

The diagnostic phase involves an assessment of four elements: policy, attitudes, current planning and regulatory system, and hot spots. Each is described below.

Policy. Ideally, local policies already establish a foundation for embarking on regulatory reform. But if support for New Urbanism is not yet established and clearly embodied in the local comprehensive plan, major zoning reform may be premature or may need to be undertaken in concert with a comprehensive planning or visioning process.

Attitudes. Interviews may be needed to assess community dynamics and attitudes. Listening to the concerns of builders and developers as well as residents, preservationists, and local businesspeople makes it possible to take stock of community attitudes and local receptivity to innovation. New Urbanist or other innovative approaches may have been tried in the past—positive results will need to be built on and negative results overcome.

Current planning and regulatory system. Conduct a careful examination to determine ways in which the current system is or is not conducive to New Urbanist development. This analysis should include comprehensive plans, regional plans, existing zoning, subdivision regulations, road specifications, environmental requirements, and the availability of infrastructure (water, sewer, roads, transit) to support New Urbanist development. How does the present system respond to good proposals and to bad ones? Can a proposal for a traditional neighborhood development or a New Urbanist infill project be easily reviewed and approved? Or do development standards thwart traditional urbanism and encourage sprawl? How do land development regulations comport with the vision expressed in the local comprehensive plan? (For some guidelines about how to audit a local comprehensive plan and regulations to see how they either permit or prohibit New Urbanist development, see PAS Report 512, *Smart Growth Audits*, by Jerry Weitz.)

Hot spots/near-term opportunities. Map those locations in the community with high levels of (re)development activity or with major sites soon to be available for development or redevelopment. Can New Urbanism be achieved in these areas under existing regulations? Or will such areas be "lost" to conventional suburban development if regulatory reform is not enacted soon? This inventory might create a checklist of conditions for each distinctive area, noting, for example:

• whether it is an infill, greenfield, or redevelopment site;

• the prevailing character and density of the area (some New Urbanist practitioners make reference to the six zones of the rural-to-urban "transect" summarized on page 36);

• the parcel pattern; and

• recent development activity either favoring or precluding New Urbanism.

STEP 2:
Determining Whether Interim Regulations Are Needed

Focusing on the hot spots identified in Step 1, assess the time dimension and the degree of imminent threat of sprawl or other inappropriate forms of development, such as big-box retail in a walkable downtown or adjoining a transit station. Sometimes drafting new plans and adopting new ordinances takes too long to prevent the loss of significant parts of the community to conventional suburban development or other development that will thwart good urbanism, particularly if there is a strong development economy. Consider some kind of an interim ordinance (typically a kind of partial moratorium) to stop or slow undesirable development and allow some form of New Urbanism (usually by some variation on the PUD process) while a new ordinance is being prepared and adopted. This is the approach Seattle took when it adopted its 1999 Interim Land Use Controls while completing work on zoning for planned transit station areas. Huntersville, North Carolina, one of the communities with an ordinance profiled in Chapter 3, enacted a full moratorium during which a new comprehensive plan was developed.

STEP 3:
Selecting Approaches to Accomplish Desired Goals

The best way to work successfully to implement New Urbanist objectives throughout a jurisdiction is to devise a set of regulatory and complementary nonregulatory actions that address the different needs of distinct parts of the municipality. These actions will have to work within the local legal and political constraints that are a fact of life. This will generally mean amending the existing code in a phased approach that ultimately infuses the entire code with New Urbanist provisions. This approach contrasts with the very ambitious strategy of attempting to adopt an entirely new code at a single time (though this has been done in a small number of locations and is considered below), the more modest one of relying on the appeal of optional provisions with accompanying incentives, or mandating New Urbanism in a limited geographic area such as an historic downtown.

With a clear list of regulatory essentials, community leaders still have a wide array of techniques they can use to implement New Urbanism. The survey and examples presented in Chapter 3 and Appendix A are testimony to the many ways that communities across the country have changed their regulations in order to incorporate New Urbanism. Increasingly, communities are finding that "the best way" involves multiple approaches. The results of the diagnostic tasks in Step 1, tailored to the specific conditions in different parts of town, can be used to create a priority list of areas needing attention. Some of these (e.g., two Main Street shopping districts or several major arterials lined with strip commercial) may be grouped together based on similar circumstances and ultimately mapped with the same district provisions. Others may be unique due to their location, size, pattern of blocks and lots, or environmental features. Once the needs of the various places are recognized, it will be time to select the regulatory interventions that will ultimately put New Urbanist regulations into effect throughout the locality. The material in this PAS Report is offered to help illustrate the characteristics, strengths, and weaknesses of the various approaches.

The job of reforming land development regulations throughout a municipality is a significant challenge, and local efforts have to be programmed accordingly. Rewriting a code into a New Urbanist format all at once is often impractical, for reasons of time, budget, and/or community acceptance. In such cases, a phased approach can be used that focuses on the areas identified in Step 1 as having the greatest threat of poor-quality development and/or the

What has it been like to try to implement these codes?

Without tremendous political support and will, it's almost impossible to make a New Urbanist code that's mandatory 100 percent of the time. You get a hybrid code that doesn't do as well. Inertia is the other problem. Developers fear that an alternative code is practically mandatory, that staff will hold them to the alternative code all the time. Developers and designers who have always worked in a certain way fear that they won't be able to design to the new code, and so they'll lose out to other developers and designers.

What are the biggest misunderstandings you come across?

The biggest is the concern over density. Density is a bad word, and rightfully so, given the kind of high-density housing that most people see. There is a lot of concern about street patterns, congestion, and cut-through traffic. These all make sense—the concerns are based on the reference point of conventional suburban development, which creates these problems. It's tough to conceive that there might be a different way of fixing problems—an entirely different way of developing communities that prevents the traffic in the first place.

You deal with it through education. Last year, I did 125 community presentations, and they were all based on the Charter of the New Urbanism. We get videos from around the country and show them on our public access TV station. The planning department now has a design studio to work with and teach developers.

The best education is to have a project on the ground. The second, third, and fourth developments are easier than the first. Once the first is there, developers, engineers, and planners can understand it, and they get excited. Our first developer learned on a tour of Florida New Urbanism. He was able to ask questions at Celebration, and then came back and started work. Once a project is on the ground, people can get out and kick the tires.

continued on page 28

What needs to change to bring New Urbanist codes into play?

The big problem is often the culture of the planning department. Planning has become a reactive discipline. People are used to reviewing subdivision requests, but they have no vision of how to help the community influence what is built.

Here in Nashville, we revamped our small area community planning process to be a charrette-based system for individual neighborhoods. We divide up the region into smaller areas, and then divide each area into neighborhoods. For each neighborhood, we have workshops that allow us to find out what people really want.

We also added a design studio to our urban planning department. At the top, we spend time figuring out how these pieces go together at the regional scale, and then we go to the neighborhood, district, and corridor scale. Now we are fixing the zoning code to make it easy for people to build to the planning goals.

continued on page 33

greatest opportunity for New Urbanism to succeed. This approach was used in the rewrite of the Green Bay, Wisconsin, zoning code, focusing on the city's older traditional neighborhoods, where contextual standards were needed; the downtown and riverfront, where mixed-use development appeared feasible; and neighborhood commercial districts, encouraging mixed use at a smaller scale. A "floating" traditional neighborhood development (TND) district was also provided for use on the city's developing fringe or larger redevelopment sites, to be mapped in conjunction with an actual development proposal. By concentrating first on critical areas like these and devising solutions that work for them, a locality can acquire experience in the application of New Urbanist approaches, solve some of its most pressing problems, and produce some good examples early in the overall regulatory reform program.

The program should also recognize that regulations won't do it all. Complementary actions needed to make the plan succeed may include public infrastructure standards, budgets, and extension policies (e.g., sewer and water lines, street improvements, school construction), as well as identification and protection of parkland or open space.

Importantly, various approaches to reform are not mutually exclusive; rather, they can be used in combination concurrently or sequentially. Three different approaches can be characterized as:

- *Area-specific regulation.* Policy and regulation applicable to a defined geographic area.
- *Strategic regulatory intervention.* Changes to portions of zoning and related codes in order to insert New Urbanist provisions.
- *Comprehensive regulatory reform.* Adoption of new land development regulations for the entire municipality.

Each is discussed below in further detail.

STEP 4: Draft Amendments to Regulations

After working through the preliminary steps, drafting regulations can begin. The provisions described in Chapter 1 should be used to amend existing regulations using the selected approaches and following the drafting principles described on the next page. The mechanics of drafting a text-based zoning ordinance are covered well in PAS Report 460, *Preparing a Conventional Zoning Ordinance*, by Charles Lerable. Of course, when preparing new sections of an existing ordinance, the drafter must determine how best to introduce new ideas in straightforward language consistent with the ordinance's established format and style.

CRAFTING YOUR APPROACH TO REGULATORY REFORM

Unfortunately, a firm commitment to principles doesn't automatically pave a clear path to a particular implementation approach. The diagnostic phase described above will help focus on options that are a good fit with the local situation. An appreciation of the possibilities of using multiple approaches in a phased or overlapping strategy will also help clarify the options. The discussions below focus on a number of key choices for crafting a local approach to regulatory reform. The case studies in Chapter 3 illuminate how some communities have successfully made these reforms.

Area-Specific Regulations

If the diagnostic effort has highlighted a small number of major development sites, you may choose to focus first on putting into place detailed site-specific regulation.

CODE DRAFTING PRINCIPLES

Here are practical drafting tips for writing legally effective New Urbanist land-use regulations (i.e. codes, ordinances, bylaws, local laws). As shown in the right-hand columns below, many of these apply to the drafting of any land-use regulation, and some are more specific to issues involving the New Urbanism. The emphasis is on the drafting of ordinances designed to promote or require New Urbanism throughout a community (as opposed to project-specific codes).

Code Drafting Principles	Universal	Specific to New Urbanism
1. State the legal authority for regulations, which is derived from state enabling legislation (zoning, subdivision, home rule, planning, etc.), and make sure that the regulations comply with state and federal law.	Yes	
2. Use terminology in a manner consistent with state law.	Yes	
3. Make clear the relationship between new code material and the existing body of land-use regulation.	Yes	
4. Make the fewest changes necessary to adequately implement New Urbanist objectives. As discussed in Chapter 2 of this PAS Report, in some cases, strategic interventions in the existing code may be sufficient, and in other cases a rewrite of an entire ordinance may be necessary.		Yes
5. Repeal or phaseout inconsistent, superfluous, or confusing code provisions from the existing code. Deletions can be as important as additions.	Yes	
6. Refer to a master plan (both comprehensive and specific plans, if possible) that provides the rationale to support the regulations.	Yes	
7. Do not use "model" provisions without adapting them to ensure that they fit the specific conditions and objectives of the community, have a logical and legally clear place in the existing framework of regulations, and comply with state law.	Yes	
8. Make regulatory language clear and precise; conceptual and abstract design language is appropriate only in plan documents and guidelines.	Yes	
9. Define New Urbanist terminology clearly, avoiding where possible the jargon of architecture and planning.		Yes
10. Avoid using regulatory language in definitions. Use definitions to define and regulations to regulate.	Yes	
11. Ensure consistency of terminology and content within each document and among all planning and regulatory documents.	Yes	
12. Explain graphics clearly in captions and text, and specify their regulatory purpose (i.e. to illustrate, explain, mandate, or to offer optional guidelines). Strike the right balance between text and graphics so that they explain each other effectively.	Yes	
13. Minimize administrative and political obstacles to New Urbanism by making approvals nondiscretionary where possible. This may require highly detailed and specific regulatory provisions, including "regulating plans." Delegate decisions to staff where practical and consistent with state law.		Yes
14. Where there are discretionary approval processes, provide clear standards to guide decision makers.	Yes	
15. Procedures for relief from decisions must afford due process to both applicants and other aggrieved parties, including a remedy if those who administer the code do not follow it.	Yes	
16. Keep regulations as simple as possible to communicate clearly and precisely with a variety of readers, especially those who will be using them most (planning commissioners, planning staff, developers, and the engineers, attorneys, and architects who represent them).	Yes	
17. Remember that regulations won't do it all: complement them with other actions needed to make the plan work, such as public street standards, public improvement budgets, and extension policies for public infrastructure (e.g. sewer and water lines, transit, school construction), as well as open space preservation programs.		Yes

From Planned Unit Developments (PUDs) to Traditional Neighborhood Developments (TNDs). It is much easier to implement a brand new code for a single development site than to reform regulations throughout the municipality. This is how the vast majority of large New Urbanist projects have been accomplished. The PUD process has typically been used as the vehicle for these projects. Early users of this approach proposed New Urbanist standards for their projects, which were often at odds with the conventional zoning in place, and which were then approved as PUDs uniquely formulated for their sites. Many noted New Urbanist projects, such as the Baldwin Park project in Orlando, Florida, which reclaimed the decommissioned Naval Training Center, and Southern Village in Chapel Hill, North Carolina, used this regulatory device. The PUD process, however, is fundamentally about providing flexibility, not about achieving New Urbanist objectives.

The PUD process offers a way to create development patterns not permitted under conventional zoning, but its openness makes possible deeply flawed results, in part because of the subjectivity in the plan review process. New Urbanist town planner Victor Dover writes about the pitfalls of the PUD process:

> Municipalities large and small are wowed by slick presentations and then badly misjudge the quality of plans. The proposals are poorly visualized. The impacts of proposals are poorly foreseen. Remember, the same discretionary process that lets a developer propose an "improved approach" lets the local government approve an inferior one. . . . The PUD process, which usually requires an upfront investment in planning and legal experts, written and graphic exhibits, and considerable time, actually favors the mightiest developers who have the money and influence it takes to get approved.

As New Urbanist practice has evolved and been championed by more and more local governments, municipalities have increasingly incorporated regulatory options for site-specific New Urbanist projects into their zoning ordinances. These continue to offer considerable flexibility in site planning, but they also contain New Urbanist standards with which the project must comply. These are most often TND districts with detailed Master Plans like PUDs. They are often more complex than PUDs and may, as in the example from Columbus, Ohio, described in Chapter 3, be adopted within the zoning code as a number of separate new districts, each of which addresses one of the component parts of a complete neighborhood.

Most TND codes require a planning process that includes two steps: first, rezoning to TND, and second, a Master Site Plan (similar to the Regulating Plan described below) to govern future site-specific development. The two steps are sometimes combined into one, with a completed Master Plan adopted concurrent with rezoning. Some jurisdictions (e.g., Gainesville, Florida, and San Antonio, Texas) allow TND by right in certain locations in order to avoid the need for rezoning, thus reducing processing time and uncertainty.

Experience with TNDs that function as optional floating zones has led to a number of different applications of the concept, all created to support development of neighborhoods with the best qualities of urbanism. While the TND approach was originally used in the context of urban expansion (i.e., "greenfield" sites), it has since been extended to redevelopment contexts as either mandatory zoning or a development option (see the St. Paul, Minnesota, example in Chapter 3). Increasingly, localities are adopting one or more mapped TND base districts in locations where the locality wishes to promote TND. In Chesapeake City, Maryland, for example, the Traditional Neighborhood base district is mapped in two urban expansion areas, while a TND floating zone is also available at the option of landowners.

THREE BASIC ZONING TERMS

Understanding these terms will help in determining which techniques should be used to implement New Urbanism; see also PAS Report No. 521/522, *A Planners Dictionary*, edited by Mike Davidson and Faye Dolnick. Note that the terms "district" and "zone" are essentially synonymous in general zoning usage.

base district   The zoning district mapped for a specific location.

overlay zone   Zoning districts that impose special regulations applied in combination with the regulations of one or more base districts to properties mapped within a specific area or meeting specified criteria (e.g., location within a floodplain or historic district). Such zones may be mandatory or optional:

- A mandatory overlay zone is most often created for the purpose of protecting specified features and resources and imposing restrictions in areas such as floodplains, aquifer recharge zones, or historic districts.

- An optional overlay zone appears on the zoning map to add flexibility rather than restriction to the underlying zoning. A mapped traditional neighborhood development zone, for example, that allows development under a set of "parallel" provisions at the option of the developer is an example of an optional zone.

floating zone   A zoning district included in the text of the zoning ordinance, but not mapped in any specific locations until applications for development meeting the districts' standards are approved. At the request of the applicant the floating zone effectively replaces the base district.

Specific Plans and Regulating Plans. PUDs and TNDs create a structure for detailed site planning to be undertaken for properties in single ownership or held by cooperating landowners. Developers typically are the ones who prepare the Master Plans mandated by PUD and TND ordinances. An alternative regulating mechanism authorized in some states by enabling legislation is the Specific Plan, which also provides for a detailed Master Plan but can address multiple properties held by multiple owners and is usually prepared by the public agency.

The Specific Plan approach has proven to be an extremely effective New Urbanist implementation technique, in part because it transcends the normal boundaries between the urban elements generally regulated separately (e.g., elements regulated in the zoning ordinance but not in the subdivision ordinance and vice versa). Implementation of New Urbanism does not observe conventional distinctions between zoning, subdivision regulation, private deed covenant and restrictions, public and private design regulation, street design and improvement, and the layout, design, construction, and maintenance of a wide range of public improvements, including sidewalks, open spaces, plantings, utilities, transit systems, and public buildings. Integration of all of these is possible within a Specific Plan or a New Urbanist Regulating Plan offering similar content.

The Regulating Plan, which is similar in content to a Specific Plan, is one of the primary tools used for implementing New Urbanism on large sites where there are multiple property owners. It uses a series of maps and text provisions with a detailed plan to govern a specific geographic area. A Regulating Plan covering the essential elements of New Urbanism will address:

- the street, alley, and block structure;

- requirements for build-to lines, yards and building massing;

- the horizontal and vertical mixing of uses;
- the placement of street trees and other natural elements;
- parking locations and requirements;
- the location of squares, greens, plazas, parks, and civic buildings (which may be public or private);
- architectural standards addressing building type and basic elements, rather than detailed design; and
- use, with standards that are relatively flexible.

Chapter 3 highlights the Regulating Plan for Central Hercules in the San Francisco Bay Area as an example of this technique. California and Arizona have enabling statutes addressing the preparation of Specific Plans. Florida's State Growth Management statute allows the same thing, calling it a Sector Plan. In other states, cities may use a similar Master Plan process, though it may not be formally codified.

A Regulating Plan for site-specific New Urbanist implementation has the the following advantages.

- It integrates all of the relevant policies, regulations, and standards for a given neighborhood or district into a single document, consolidating different types of regulations usually covered in separate ordinances.

- It usually applies to multiple properties with different owners and does not necessitate property owner agreement, as does a PUD.

- By incorporating the zoning for the area it covers, a Regulating Plan can eliminate the necessity for multiple rezonings or overlay districts.

- It tells landowners and the public exactly what a community wants in a particular location, using graphic material to communicate as much as possible, providing clarity, certainty, and predictability.

The preparation of Regulating Plans can be costly and time consuming, although once one or a few Regulating Plans are written, many of the elements in one can be "plugged in" to another, saving time and money. Costs can also be viewed as upfront community investments in a process that will later streamline development approvals resulting in savings. While detailed site-specific zoning is simpler than conventional zoning in some ways, it can result in an increase in regulations overall if multiple Regulating Plans are adopted to cover a variety of areas in the jurisdiction. Communities need to carefully consider the use and possible abuse of the Regulating Plan approach.

A Regulating Plan needs to be flexible enough to accommodate typical changes in market conditions or external forces over time. A procedure for minor revisions to the plan without requiring new approvals should be established.

Overall, a Regulating Plan adopted through a Specific Plan mechanism is probably the most effective technique available to implement New Urbanist planning in a focused area. It enables land-use regulation to move from abstract general categories and numerical parameters to site-specific planning and design based upon the context, location, and unique circumstances of each site. An updated zoning ordinance intended to implement New Urbanism would be well-served by including a process for developing and adopting Regulating Plans based upon New Urbanist principles.

Strategic Regulatory Intervention

Many community leaders want to act quickly to make their land-use regulations implement New Urbanism. By translating key principles into specific regulatory changes, a community can start to change its development pattern without having to completely overhaul its code. These strategic interventions may be put into place relatively quickly so change begins in the near term—perhaps while comprehensive regulatory reform or detailed area-specific planning efforts are underway. If the political commitment to New Urbanism is in place, communities can make significant changes to their regulations while avoiding a complex, technical, and time-consuming process.

One common approach to incorporating New Urbanism into zoning is to make strategic changes in existing zoning districts, altering use provisions, dimensional regulations, and supplementary regulations to embody New Urbanist principles. Included among the actions in Chapter 1 are relatively simple but strategic interventions that can make a zoning ordinance significantly more New Urbanist in its approach. This is the least radical intervention, but it can produce significant results, particularly if the overall structure and language of the zoning code is relatively sound. Look at what exists in the community in specific neighborhoods and areas. Is it already close to the New Urbanist approach? If so, tweaking regulation may be all that is necessary in those areas. Use illustrations of existing buildings (e.g., the Woodford County, Kentucky, approach; see the illustration on page 14 in Chapter 1), neighborhoods, and developments that are examples of good urbanism so that citizens and political leaders can literally see what the consequences of the regulations will be. It may even be possible to adopt regulations of one existing community area and apply them to others. Such strategic intervention without complex overhauls is not adequate where the primary objective is to address the complex challenges of suburban retrofit or protection of rural character—for these situations, a more complex approach is likely to be needed. The strategic intervention approach can also be used during an interim period while a more comprehensive regulatory revision process is underway, serving as a stopgap to prevent further degradation of the community.

Comprehensive Regulatory Reform

An ordinance ready for a complete overhaul presents an excellent opportunity for the incorporation of New Urbanist principles throughout its content and throughout the jurisdiction. This approach can be the most costly and time-consuming, but it is also the most thorough and effective way to accomplish New Urbanism. A number of smaller communities around the country, such as Cornelius, Davidson, and Huntersville, North Carolina, have developed complete new ordinances. San Antonio, Texas, has pioneered a hybrid Unified Development Code that incorporates New Urbanist provisions throughout and also offers options for specific types of projects with a strong New Urbanist character. Milwaukee, Wisconsin, is another large city that has made many revisions throughout its ordinance to incorporate New Urbanist policies. A revised ordinance may include Regulating Plans for specific areas that are the focus of major government initiatives or private-sector activity, or it may include procedures for devising future Regulating Plans in locations where they are most desirable.

Optional or Mandatory Approaches

Some localities avoid the many difficulties of the existing regulatory framework by adopting a "parallel" code applying to the same properties. The local government applies the parallel code's provisions only when the developer who wants to build in the area requests that the development be governed by the provisions in that parallel code. The local government generally provides incentives in the form of expedited approvals and permits to encourage developers to use the parallel code. This approach has been taken in Austin, Texas, Dade County, Florida, and Columbus, Ohio. It is also the basis for the model TND ordinance prepared in Wisconsin under state mandate.

How do you use incentives for New Urbanism?

We don't use incentives. We don't need to bribe people to do the right thing. By nature, a New Urbanist code allows more density, narrower streets, and mixed use in order to accomplish its goals. They are not incentives, but they all help the developer make more money.

In Orlando, we had traffic impact fees. If a developer followed the New Urbanist code, the impact fees were 30 to 35 percent lower. This wasn't an incentive either, but rather recognition of the different travel patterns and modes in a New Urbanist neighborhood.

Some places try to provide faster processing for developers following the New Urbanist code, but we try to process everything pretty fast, so that's less of an issue.

Market demand is not enough to get the first couple of developments built. You have to make it easy for them. But after that, market demand takes over.

What do you mandate in New Urbanist development?

Once you have a parallel code, it's full of mandatory requirements for those who follow it. It has build-to lines, location of parking, number and location of door openings, and block size, for example. With a parallel code, you put in whatever you want. But to make it useful for developers and for the city, you have to decide: Do we need to mandate fenestration details? How important is a particular architectural style? Usually, you can do without some of those. What matters is what lasts: public space, massing, access, and streets.

How do you get developers to provide mixed housing types in a development?

It's not an issue. Most projects have mixed housing types. Two projects are underway in Nashville, and both have a wide range of prices. The downtown project has a developer who was committed to affordable housing, and the greenfield project includes live-work, single-family homes, and an area set aside for multifamily development.

continued on page 36

As is reported in Chapter 3, there are some circumstances in which the parallel code approach is working as intended, but numerous others where there has been no development. The advantages of using a parallel code are that it avoids having to deal with the complexities of the existing code and can offer a streamlined alternative for motivated developers. Also, the processing incentives give New Urbanist projects a better position from which to compete in the marketplace with conventional development.

PUTTING THE PUBLIC PROCESS TO WORK

By Gianni Longo

Public involvement started as a protest movement. Citizens organized against planning decisions they felt affected them negatively. Targets for this type of organized protest were typically the decisions to run highways through neighborhoods, the displacement of low-income residents from urban renewal areas, and all kinds of environmental degradation.

Today, while some of the opposition to projects remains very much a part of the public process in the form of Not In My Backyard (NIMBY) activism, a great deal of public involvement occurs through carefully designed participatory activities. These activities start early in the planning process and continue throughout the development of the plan and the adoption process. Needless to say, a plan developed with strong community support is more likely to be swiftly adopted and implemented because the public involvement will capture the attention of decision makers.

Several public participation techniques have proven valuable in facilitating public buy-in in the development of a plan. They include, among others, visioning, visual preference surveys, and charrettes. There are many reasons for the acceptance of these techniques in the planning process. They work well in translating ideas into physical plan elements, are well liked by participants (as identified in a variety of follow-up studies), and are designed to reach clearly understood outcomes that work well in support of various aspects of a plan. These techniques are often used together to accomplish specific goals of a plan.

Visioning is typically a process designed to create a foundation of agreement in support of the elements of a plan. It works well as a tool to develop a comprehensive plan, and it is practically the only way to develop a regional plan. In a visioning process, participants go through several steps, including brainstorming about the future, organizing ideas generated through the brainstorming, and developing goals and strategies supported by those ideas.

A visual preference survey is visioning that measures participants' preferences toward existing and possible patterns of development. It works extremely well in support of design guidelines and in the identification of preferred development scenarios. Visual preference surveys use photographs, computer-generated graphics, and 3-D models as the tools to trigger participants responses.

Charrettes are concentrated multidisciplinary planning or design activities, and their use is an important part of New Urbanist practice. In a short period of time, typically a week, a charrette can produce highly developed design alternatives and plans that have citizen buy-in. In the public involvement part of a charrette, citizen and stakeholder work as teams with designers and planners and use maps and drawings to develop design alternatives for a given area of a community.

Elected and appointed officials can play a key role in these types of public participation processes as members of ad-hoc governance structures by providing input at key junctures. Their visibility in the process makes for a smoother transition between the development, adoption, and implementation phases of the plan.

The disadvantages are that it:

- typically does not address the entire range of issues in a community;

- will not be used by those who do not understand or appreciate New Urbanism;

- may become buried in the ordinance along with many other optional seldom-used provisions; and

- will not be used in areas where conventional suburban development is more profitable for a developer.

The gravest danger, though, is that providing New Urbanism solely as an option encourages the continuation of the very development patterns that we are trying to transform, allowing more and more land to be developed conventionally and exacerbating the problems created by late-twentieth-century zoning practice.

The parallel code can be an important part of a multiphase regulatory reform program. Far easier to adopt than mandatory new base districts, a parallel code can sometimes be put into effect quickly. This approach will allow New Urbanist projects to move forward while a long-term effort incorporates New Urbanism into the ordinance's mandatory provisions.

The parallel code can be an important part of a multiphase regulatory reform program.

CONVENTIONAL FORMATS, NEW STANDARDS (OR "NEW WINE IN OLD BOTTLES")

Conventional zoning has been a major perpetrator of sprawl. This may result more from an ordinance's content than its format. The often wordy, redundant, and legalistic nature of many conventional ordinances, however, has also drawn much criticism. Ordinances that are difficult to use or interpret tend to discourage creative approaches to development. Despite these difficulties, many localities want to change the outcomes of the development process while retaining a conventional zoning format, finding that building on a familiar format can be the best way to get results.

Numerous communities have adopted new base districts that emphasize a mix of uses, employing New Urbanist dimensional standards, with greater emphasis on design and less on use. Boulder, Colorado, has achieved notable results through a transformation of its conventional zoning regulations, which retained their format while changing their content. Many other communities are taking a similar approach, as documented in Appendix A.

The mixed-use building at 15th and Pearl in Boulder, Colorado, realizes many New Urbanist principles, creating a pedestrian-friendly streetfront on the ground floor while providing a five-level parking structure above. Boulder made strategic interventions in its zoning ordinance to achieve these ends without rewriting its entire code.

How do you put the Transect into law?

The Transect (see the section opposite and the illustration on page 37) is the core of our planning effort. We start with the Transect at the citywide level. We identify what Transect level each part of the city is. Then we go to the neighborhood level and use it to get detailed and refined. A T-4 neighborhood, for example, might have small parts that are core, center, general, and edge. Those detailed levels of Transect analysis are used for zoning.

There are core, center, general, and edge areas in each of T-4, T-5, and T-6. In T-3, it is mostly edge. In T-2 and T-3, there might be centers, but they are different from other centers.

For some parts of planning, the neighborhood Transect zone is all you need. For our bicycle and pedestrian plan, or for our parks plan, we identify certain needs in T-4 neighborhoods that are less important in T-3 neighborhoods. For example, you don't have neighborhood parks in a T-3 neighborhood, since there is more private open space. You do in T-4. You don't necessarily have sidewalks on every street in T-3, but you do in T-4. T-5, in turn, has different sidewalks and parks guidelines.

In short, we identify areas by Transect zone, but we don't zone them with a uniform "T-3 zoning," for example. We give them a zoning package that is consistent with T-3.

How can New Urbanists improve the integration of the whole development management system?

Coordination is important. In Orlando, we had planning, code enforcement, building permits, and even Community Development Block Grant funding all in one department. In Nashville, planners have to work with those other departments to ensure that they understand what we mean in our plans and are permitting the right kinds of places.

NEW APPROACHES

Form-based Zoning

Many New Urbanist practitioners work to achieve different outcomes by using both new formats and new standards. The dominant new approach is form-based, making building type, street type, or a combination of the two the primary regulatory elements. The Columbia Pike Form-Based Development Regulations described in Chapter 3 are an example of the form-based or typological zoning approach. This approach generally combines the features of a Regulating Plan with a set of building envelope standards governing height, siting, building elements (e.g., windows and entries), and use for a number of building types. New Urbanist Peter Katz explains that "form-based coding is founded on the idea that a community's physical 'form' is its most intrinsic and enduring characteristic" and that form "includes not just buildings and blocks, but a constellation of physical elements that may include public spaces such as streets, squares, and greenbelts; civic infrastructure such as canals, bridges, and drainage systems; and natural features such as lakes, riparian corridors and beaches." Form-based zoning approaches can also be used within the framework of a conventionally structured ordinance, supplementing or replacing sections dealing with dimensional, design, and street standards.

Transect-Based Zoning

New Urbanists have begun to use the urban-rural "transect" as a classification system or organizing principle for planning and zoning. In the natural sciences, transects are geographical cross-sections used to survey areas. In urban design and planning, the transect approach is applied to built as well as natural environments by New Urbanist architect and town planner Andres Duany. The transect system classifies six zones using typical elements of natural and built habitats, ranging from most rural to most urban. The zones are: T1: natural; T2: rural; T3: suburban; T4: general urban; T5: urban center; and T6: urban core.

One of the key concepts of transect planning and zoning is the idea of creating what are called "immersive environments"—places where various physical characteristics of buildings, landscape, and the public realm combine to create a coherent sense of place. They vary in intensity of use from the most rural (T1) to the most urban (T6). All zones, however, contain a mix of uses with the density, intensity, and design characteristics depending upon the degree to which the area is rural or urban. An essential aspect of planning based on the transect system is creating a proper balance between natural and human environments along the rural to urban transect. Avoiding the urbanizing of the rural, such as placing office towers in suburbs or, equally damaging, ruralizing the urban, is another aspect of using a transect system.

Duany Plater-Zyberk and Company have developed a model transect-based code, known as the Smart Code. The code begins with a list of the basic principles of good urban form and then proceeds with specific sets of standards that vary from one transect zone to another. The standards address:

- *building disposition,* specifying lot size, frontage, and setback requirements for each zone;
- *building configuration,* specifying frontage type (e.g., porch, stoop, or gallery) and building height;
- *building function,* which indicates the uses prescribed for each transect zone;
- *parking;*

- *street sections;*
- *architecture;*
- *landscaping; and*
- *signage.*

Applying standards to each transect zone is a matter of specifying the degree of urban intensity appropriate to that zone. A few general guidelines give a sense of what this entails. At the rural end of the continuum, standards call for:

- less density;
- smaller, detached buildings;
- deep setbacks;
- paths, trails;
- open swales;
- country roads; and
- irregular plantings.

At the most urban end of the continuum, standards call for

- higher density;
- larger, attached buildings;
- shallow setbacks;
- street and alley sections;
- a formal street grid;
- wide sidewalks; and
- formal plantings.

As one moves along the transect from rural to urban conditions, the density and complexity of human elements increases while the density and complexity of natural elements decreases.

You also need to work with the fire, public works, water, and sewer departments, or they will stop developers from creating the kinds of places you want. We are bringing in transportation engineers to talk to the transportation engineers and bringing in fire experts to talk with the fire chief. That way they can talk about the technical questions they have. I've found that once they see what you're talking about, they get excited and want to do this kind of work.

You also have to work with the public. It's not about showing them how wrong they are.

You need to show them that similar people, with the same concerns, have done this kind of development in other places.

What is the most important tool for implementing a New Urbanist code?

Education. You need to keep people learning, both inside and outside the planning department, so you can deal with fears. You can show that New Urbanism will not cause property values to go to hell, and the world is not ending. You can use examples from the places people know and love, usually within your city or town. That way people will be much more excited about this form of development. ■

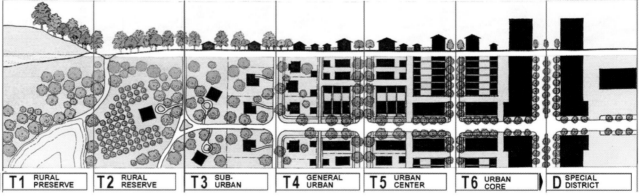

Source: Duany Plater-Zyberk

The six transect zones are diagrammed in idealized form in this illustration. In real places, the zones are often found in complex patterns rather than in a continuum.

CHAPTER 3

From Building to Region:
New Urbanist Regulations in Place

by Ellen Greenberg, AICP

American zoning has historically concerned itself not with the positive contributions of buildings to their community but with the avoidance of negative impacts. The essence of zoning has been its attention to site and building. Now, many localities are transcending this narrow approach with regard to both reach and scale.

The Charter of the New Urbanism's 27 principles are organized into three scales, thus illuminating the links between building and region as well as highlighting elements addressed uniquely at one scale or another. A fundamental obstacle to implementing the New Urbanism is that the scales used to organize the principles have no parallels in the legal framework that enables the regulation of land development.

The finest of the Charter scales—addressing the block, the street and the building—finds immediate parallels in standard zoning and is clearly envisioned in enabling statutes. By contrast, the largest—the region, metropolis, city, and town—is at odds with modern American zoning practice, though a small number of cities, perhaps most notably San Diego, California, have used zoning to implement comprehensive growth management policies addressing regional form. Of course, municipal zoning is geographically comprehensive in that it typically addresses all properties within the jurisdiction. It often fails to do so, however, in a way that is functionally comprehensive; namely, a way that uses zoning as a tool to implement the environmental, economic, social, and cultural relationships addressed in the Charter.

THE REGION: METROPOLIS, CITY, AND TOWN

How can regional principles, such as encouraging infill development over peripheral expansion and organizing noncontiguous development as distinct towns and villages, be effectively implemented in the absence of regulating authority by regional bodies? Committed government agencies and independent organizations are finding ways to address these issues, stretching the limits of standard tools and sometimes crafting new ones. CNU's survey of New Urbanist regulations yields a surprising array of ways that regional principles are being advanced through land development regulation. The unifying element is that direct regulation of land use and development remains the purview of local government.

The following techniques are being used to integrate the Charter's regional principles into land development regulation.

Large-Scale Planning and Focused Regulation

A number of very-large-scale planning and regulatory efforts undertaken within a single jurisdiction are addressing regional issues including resource protection, jobs/housing relationships, and affordable housing. The Orlando Southeast Sector Plan highlighted below serves as both a policy and regulatory document for 19,300 acres of new growth area.

Regionally Consistent Regulations

From North Carolina come the most prominent examples of localities working in concert to incorporate New Urbanist principles into their separate ordinances. Two areas of the state demonstrate two approaches. In Cabarrus County, the county and four municipal governments have all agreed to adopt similar unified development ordinances and to conduct quarterly updates revising the codes in response to their experiences applying it. The county is responsible for adopting the ordinance, which will regulate development on unincorporated lands. By contrast, four communities having jurisdiction over approximately 100 square miles of high-growth area near Charlotte are working in concert without a formal agreement. Huntersville, Cornelius, and Davidson, North Carolina, all have followed the earlier lead of neighboring Belmont in adopting New Urbanist regulations. The communities were greatly aided by a countywide visioning process led by David Walters of the University of North Carolina College of Architecture.

Regional Transit Investment

In some parts of the country, hundreds of millions of dollars are being spent on light rail transit without any requirements that local governments zone for densities and uses to support ridership. A few regions, however, have created needed links between local regulations and transit investments, and in so doing provide a compelling demonstration of how the Charter scales can be linked in practice. Seattle's station area planning process (Figure 3-1) and

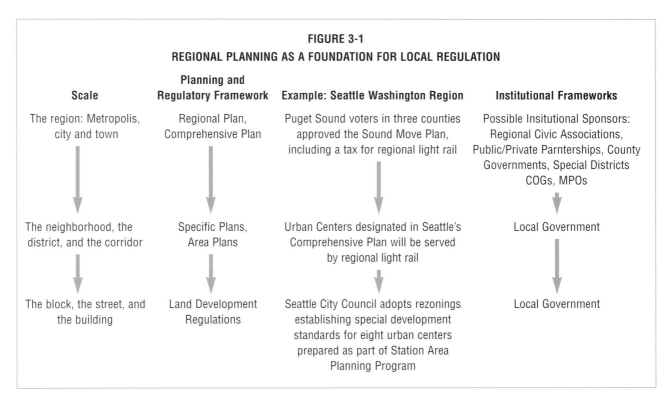

FIGURE 3-1
REGIONAL PLANNING AS A FOUNDATION FOR LOCAL REGULATION

Scale	Planning and Regulatory Framework	Example: Seattle Washington Region	Institutional Frameworks
The region: Metropolis, city and town	Regional Plan, Comprehensive Plan	Puget Sound voters in three counties approved the Sound Move Plan, including a tax for regional light rail	Possible Insitutional Sponsors: Regional Civic Associations, Public/Private Parnterships, County Governments, Special Districts COGs, MPOs
The neighborhood, the district, and the corridor	Specific Plans, Area Plans	Urban Centers designated in Seattle's Comprehensive Plan will be served by regional light rail	Local Government
The block, the street, and the building	Land Development Regulations	Seattle City Council adopts rezonings establishing special development standards for eight urban centers prepared as part of Station Area Planning Program	Local Government

examples from the Oregon communities of Gresham and Hillsboro illustrate this approach to development regulation at the Charter's largest scale.

Building Codes

The rehabilitation building codes adopted by the states of New Jersey and Maryland apply statewide and were put into place with the express objective of redirecting investment to the state's older urbanized areas, thus strengthening those established centers and reducing pressures for urban expansion.

Model Codes

Model codes offered by state governments (Wisconsin, Oregon, Maryland) or advocacy groups (Envision Utah) embody New Urbanist and smart growth principles, and offer many jurisdictions an easy, if unsystematic, implementation tool.

A model code that operates at all scales is the SmartCode, created by Duany Plater-Zyberk and Company as an alternative to zoning ordinances that encourage single-use development at the expense of neighborhood viability. Dealing with all aspects of design across the rural to urban transect—including building disposition and configuration, street and landscape standards, parking, and architecture—the SmartCode was designed for municipalities seeking to implement New Urbanist principles through local regulations. Like all model codes, the SmartCode should be customized to respond to a community's vision and goals.

THE NEIGHBORHOOD, THE DISTRICT, AND THE CORRIDOR

Many features discussed in the Charter's principles for the neighborhood, district, and corridor are typically addressed in both conventional and New Urbanist development regulations, but in different ways. Regulation of density and use are familiar to users of almost any ordinance, though the regulations profiled here are distinguished by a particular intent: implementing the principles of mixed use and walkability in compact neighborhoods. TOD regula-

The planning and regulatory process for TOD in the Seattle, Washington, region illuminates one method of linking implementation of principles at the three scales addressed in the Charter of the New Urbanism.

tions that specify density gradients correlated with distance from a rail station and TND ordinances specifying the way land is to be allocated to insure balanced neighborhoods with respect to both private and public activities specifically address the Charter's emphasis on neighborhood structure at this scale.

Because neighborhoods and districts usually are contained within single localities, the legal and institutional framework is in place to regulate at this scale. Corridors, by contrast, frequently cross jurisdictional lines (and in some important cases may have street right-of-way under the control of a road or highway agency separate from the local government). Corridors may benefit from the techniques in use by cooperative neighboring localities.

As discussed in Chapter 2, one technique that facilitates implementation at the neighborhood scale is the use of the Specific Plan. The Specific Plan is expressly authorized by state enabling legislation in California and Arizona, and takes various forms in other states. It is a document that may be adopted for areas in multiple ownerships, and it establishes both policy and regulations, replacing any existing zoning. In many cases, the Specific Plan process provides a mechanism by which local goernments can compel neighboring property owners to cooperate, thereby facilitating the implementation of neighborhood or corridorwide objectives.

One of the most familiar forms of New Urbanist development—the traditional neighborhood development (TND)—is at the middle scale addressed by the Charter. The first generations of TNDs were created almost exclusively as planned unit developments (PUDs) without any land development regulations explicitly calling for New Urbanism. As communities have come to seek out or even demand New Urbanist approaches for their major expansion, infill, and redevelopment projects, TND regulations or modified PUD procedures are increasingly governing the creation of New Urbanist neighborhoods. While many TND ordinances are limited to properties larger than 40 acres, so that all neighborhood components can be included, the Columbus, Ohio, example can be applied to properties as small as two acres. From St. Paul, Minnesota, comes a TND ordinance for use on large urban redevelopment sites that seeks to strengthen and expand the city's existing neighborhoods.

THE BLOCK, THE STREET, AND THE BUILDING

All land development regulations work at the scale of the building, though in markedly different ways and with varying levels of detail. While the building and site are the focus of conventional zoning, attention to their relationship to blocks and street and their contributions to the public realm is a defining characteristic of New Urbanist regulations. The Pasadena, California, City of Gardens regulations for multifamily housing address these relationships as well as to the use of landscape design and historic precedents. Examples of form-based codes that use street type as a central element are from Hercules, California, and Arlington County, Virginia.

Another New Urbanist practice is reducing the emphasis on regulation of use in favor of regulatory provisions that put use, design, and development standards in greater balance. The code for Huntersville, North Carolina, sets forth four sets of provisions that offer this balance, addressing use, building and lot types, street type, and miscellaneous provisions (e.g., off-street parking and sign regulation), respectively.

REAL PLACES CHANGE THE RULES:
NEW URBANIST REGULATIONS IN 12 COMMUNITIES

Regulatory innovation is happening in small and large cities across the country, belying the idea that our communities can't build places better than sprawling subdivisions. As the examples provided in this chapter show, New Urbanism has taken hold in a wide variety of places, and regulations are being crafted that meld the unique features of each place with the principles of the Charter of the New Urbanism and the techniques introduced in this PAS Report. In this chapter are summaries of land development regulations from 12 places across the U.S., ranging from village to state, that are working to implement the principles that are at the heart of the New Urbanist movement. Each of the regulations highlighted here was selected because of its attention to one or more regulatory objectives that are central to implementing the principles of New Urbanism.

The examples are organized according to their "reach" relative to the scales described in the Charter—from region to building. Those addressing regional principles, with the exception of the New Jersey example, do so, not through direct regulation, but through the use of one or more of the techniques described above.

For each example, introductory comments address key points, including:

- *techniques illustrated*—the substantive and/or procedural features that make the ordinance worthy of inclusion in this PAS Report;

- *setting and background*—information about the location where the ordinance applies, and the history of its preparation and adoption;

- *key features of the regulations*—the distinguishing provisions the community employs to implement the ordinance; and

- *meeting regulatory objectives*—namely, the objectives central to New Urbanism. In some cases, all seven of the objectives are addressed; in others, as few as two are. In the case of the examples we provide for this PAS Report, regulations had to provide either a particularly important example of a focus on a single objective (as, for example, the State of New Jersey has focused on infill and rehabilitation, or Pasadena on design context) or, as in most of the examples, to be comprehensive, meaning they address most of the New Urbanist objectives.

The cases illustrate three approaches to incorporating New Urbanist regulations locally.

1 *Parallel.* In such cases, New Urbanist regulations are adopted as an option, typically invoked at the request of the property owner. If the parallel regulations are not selected, conventional regulations remain in force. Frequently, certain requirements, such as acreage thresholds or locational criteria, must be met in order for the parallel regulations to be used.

2 *Mandatory.* The standard provisions of the zoning ordinance incorporate New Urbanist principles and apply to all development.

3 *Hybrid.* A number of localities, including Gainesville, Florida, have incorporated mandatory New Urbanist provisions in some zoning districts, and also offer a parallel option for new growth areas. These are termed "hybrid" provisions in the discussion below.

The examples vary in their approach, context, and applicability, as can be seen from the summary table in Appendix A. All had been adopted as of May 2004. Regulations that have been in place for the longest time (e.g., Pasadena's multifamily district and the downtown district from Skaneateles New York) provide a useful perspective on early efforts to alter conventional zoning ordinances by incorporating New Urbanist provisions.

While many observers associate New Urbanism with large-scale greenfield projects, the survey has yielded valuable examples of New Urbanist regulations in established urban areas. Thus, the collection includes regulations applying to a range of conditions, from the almost-20,000-acre Orlando Southeast Sector Plan and Guidelines, which address the planned urbanization of a small number of very large land holdings, to the Seattle, Washington, Station Area Overlay District, which applies to many small properties in highly urbanized neighborhoods. In Arlington County, Virginia, the new form-based code described below applies to many properties along 3.5 miles of the historic Columbia Pike.

The highlights provided here offer only a glimpse into a rich array of regulations in place and in development throughout the country. Appendix A supplements these with the results of a more extensive survey that reports on 20 additional communities with New Urbanist regulations, including information about their preparation and adoption, distinguishing characteristics, and application. For a full understanding of both general approach and specific provisions, readers will need to consult the full ordinances and related maps.

TABLE 3-2
SCALE EMPHASIZED IN ZONING CODES IN CHAPTER 3 CASE STUDIES

	The region			Neighbor-hood	District	Corridor	Block	Street	Building
	Metropolis	City	Town						
Seattle, Washington: Station Area Planning Program	▓	▓	▓	▓	▓	▓	▓	▓	▓
State of New Jersey: Uniform Construction Code Rehabilitation Subcode	▓	▓	▓	▓	▓	▓	▓	▓	▓
Orlando, Florida: Southeast Orlando Sector Plan Development Guidelines and Standards	▓	▓	▓	▓	▓	▓	▓	▓	▓
San Antonio, Texas: Unified Development Code			▓	▓	▓	▓	▓	▓	
Huntersville, North Carolina: Zoning Ordinance		▓	▓	▓	▓	▓	▓	▓	
Arlington, Virginia: Columbia Pike Special Revitalization District Form Based Code				▓	▓	▓	▓	▓	▓
Hercules, California: Regulating Code for the Central Hercules Plan				▓	▓	▓	▓	▓	▓
Petaluma, California: Central Petaluma SmartCode				▓	▓	▓	▓	▓	▓
Columbus, Ohio: Traditional Neighborhood Development Article				▓	▓	▓	▓	▓	
St. Paul, Minnesota: Urban Village Code				▓	▓	▓	▓	▓	
Skaneateles, New York: Village of Skaneateles Zoning Law				▓	▓	▓	▓	▓	
Pasadena, California: Pasadena City of Gardens							▓	▓	▓

Range of scales of the Charter of the New Urbanism addressed by each of the 12 examples presented in this chapter

NEW URBANIST REGULATORY OBJECTIVES

(The Charter's 27 principles are included in Appendix B of this PAS Report.)

Objective 1: Allow a variety of uses to create vitality and bring many activities of daily living within walking distance of homes

New Urbanist practice brings activities into proximity in the interest of convenience, walkability, and liveliness. This contrasts with the separation of uses characteristic of Euclidean zoning.

Objective 2: Foster mixed residential density and housing types

New Urbanist projects are reviving a traditional neighborhood form by mixing density and housing type within each neighborhood or block to allow households with different needs to live close together. This diversity reverses the post-war pattern of residential development in the United States characterized by uniformity of type, design, and density.

Objective 3: Stimulate infill and rehabilitation activity

Achieving the goals of New Urbanism means strengthening existing urban areas through development of vacant and underused sites and repair and renovation of older structures. This is accomplished through innovative revisions to building codes as well as zoning regulations.

Objective 4: Develop contextual design standards to ensure that new development responds to the traditional architectural styles of the city or region

Because private buildings give shape and character to the public streets and open spaces that together create the public realm that is a focus of New Urbanism, their design and placement need to be addressed in development regulations. While architectural style need not be prescribed, the Charter principles assert "architecture and landscape design should grow from local climate, topography, history, and building practice," thus avoiding the monotony of conventional suburban development and instead creating places of character and distinction.

Objective 5: Create compact, walkable centers and neighborhoods served by public transit

A mix of housing types and land uses is essential to achieving the intensity of development needed to support walkable centers and to enable public transit to operate successfully.

Objective 6: Enhance streetscapes and civic life

New Urbanist regulations include detailed provisions for streets and civic spaces, recognizing their importance in community life and placemaking. Zoning regulations administered by a planning or community development department are often complemented by street standards administered by public works departments to achieve this objective.

Objective 7: Shape metropolitan regions with public space, farmland, and natural areas

The Charter of the New Urbanism places particular emphasis on the relationship between the metropolis and its agrarian surroundings and natural landscape. Local development regulations must address the potential conflict between urbanism and environmental preservation while supporting productive agriculture, rural communities, and a clear urban/rural edge.

SEATTLE, WASHINGTON, STATION AREA PLANNING PROGRAM

Source document: Seattle Station Area Planning Program closeout report, August 15, 2001, by City of Seattle Strategic Planning Office; Station Area Overlay District (SAOD), Ordinance 120452, adopted July 2001; authored by City of Seattle planning staff

Code authors: City of Seattle Planning Staff

Staff contact: Calvin Chow, Assistant Sound Transit Program Manager, calvin.chow@seattle.gov

Web site: www.seattle.gov/transportation/ppmp_sap_council.htm

Techniques illustrated:
- Local regulations are linked to municipal, regional, and statewide planning.
- Seattle's Station Area Planning Program recognizes that transit-oriented districts (TODs) are unique because of the need to shape use and design character in a way that responds to the high level of accessibility provided by light rail. The SAOD codifies the distinguishing characteristics of transit-oriented places.
- The code uses interim standards during preparation of station area plans and regulations.
- The ordinance contains provisions addressing the nature of appropriate and inappropriate businesses and uses in a TOD.

Since the adoption of Washington State's 1990 Growth Management Act, Seattle has had an extraordinarily active planning program. Following the 1994 adoption of Seattle's Comprehensive Plan, 38 Seattle neighborhoods developed 20-year plans for their futures. In 1996, Puget Sound voters in three counties approved the Sound Move plan and in doing so agreed to tax themselves to construct a new mass transit system. More than 65 percent of Seattle voters approved the Sound Move plan, at the heart of which is Sound Transit's Link light rail. The first phase of light rail will run from the city of SeaTac north to downtown Seattle and will serve as the backbone for mass transit in Seattle. The planned light rail alignment serves four of the five urban centers designated by the comprehensive plan as well as several urban villages. Downtown Seattle, First Hill, and the University District are the three densest employment centers in the state. All will be served by the planned light rail alignment.

In 1998, the city initiated an extensive Station Area Planning (SAP) program built on the effort to integrate planned light rail investments with the visions expressed in the neighborhood plans. Sound Transit, King County, and the Puget Sound Regional Council were Seattle's partners in the SAP process. Seattle's station area zoning is an example of local regulations that support the objective of "coherent regional planning" expressed in the Charter of the New Urbanism.

Key Features of the Regulations

The implementing regulations have three parts:

1. *Rezoning in some station areas.* The city council adopted eight resolutions during 2001, addressing the mix of uses, development standards, and street characteristics, based on unique neighborhood plans.

2. *The Station Area Overlay District (SAOD).* Seattle's SAOD includes some provisions that are often overlooked in conversations about TOD and New Urbanism, but that reflect the realities of managing change in a mature urban environment. The most significant of these address the future of existing businesses and uses that may not be appropriate in a transit-oriented district. While prohibiting new auto-oriented uses, the ordinance allows all existing legal businesses and uses to remain. Some

of the uses that are made nonconforming by the overlay or associated rezoning are allowed a one-time expansion.

3. *The coordination of specific regulations with specific neighborhood plans.* The overlay district codifies a relatively small number of provisions that work in combination with underlying land-use regulations to implement the vision of each area as expressed in neighborhood plans.

Meeting Regulatory Objectives

Allowing a variety of uses. Market studies in a number of the station areas indicated demand for single-purpose residential uses in commercial zones, and SAOD makes it possible to achieve such a mix of uses. Ground-floor housing is permitted for now, with the hope for future conversion to commercial space when there is a stronger market.

Fostering mixed residential density and housing type. A residential base is required to create a vital, mixed-use town center. The overlay district provisions are intended to remove obstacles to housing development. The overlay district eases the city's usual requirements for mixed-use development by eliminating lot coverage maximums for the residential portion of mixed-use buildings.

Creating compact, walkable downtowns, and neighborhoods. Auto-oriented commercial streets around the new light rail stations have been

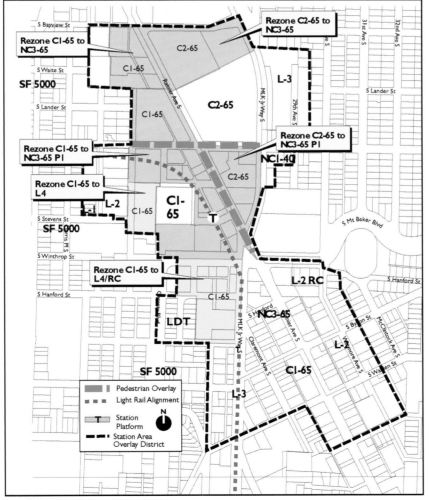

Source: SAOD & Rezone Ordinance 120455, Exhibit A

For each of the city's eight station areas, the Seattle municipal code has been amended to rezone certain properties within the area of the transit stations. Boundaries of the Station Area Overlay District are also mapped.

Existing Zones

General Commercial (C1-65)

An auto-oriented, primarily retail-service commercial area, serving surrounding neighborhoods and larger community or citywide clientele with a wide range of commercial services, including retail, offices and business support services; residential use is also permitted.
Height Limit: 65 feet

Proposed Zones

Neighborhood Commercial (NC3-65)

A pedestrian-oriented shopping district serving both surrounding neighborhood and larger community or citywide clientele with a wide range of retail businesses as well as offices and business support services. Residential use is also permitted.

Height Limit: 65 feet*Lowrise 4 (L4 and L4/RC)* Moderate density multifamily development in neighborhoods already characterized by moderate density residential structures. RC designation allows for some limited commercial use.
Height Limit: 37 feet

redesignated as pedestrian streets. That designation is expressed at the parcel level through maximum setbacks, transparency standards (e.g., windows rather than blank walls must be used at street level), and a requirement that ground-floor businesses be pedestrian-oriented.

The overlay district forbids auto-oriented businesses, such as drive-throughs, and primary parking facilities, though existing uses are allowed to remain. It adds design flexibility (especially increasing the allowable area of upper stories) and a requirement that parking be in the rear or side of buildings.

To complement the overlay, the city has rezoned lots near the stations from auto-oriented commercial to the designation "neighborhood commercial."

STATE OF NEW JERSEY DEPARTMENT OF COMMUNITY AFFAIRS
UNIFORM CONSTRUCTION CODE, REHABILITATION SUBCODE

Source document:	Information Kit, New Jersey Rehabilitation Code, New Jersey Department of Community Affairs; New Jersey Administrative Code Title 5 Chapter 23 Subchapter 6
Code authors:	State of New Jersey Department of Community Affairs
Web site:	www.state.nj.us/dca/codes/rehab/viewbysection.shtml
Techniques illustrated:	The State of New Jersey code is a pioneering building code intended to stimulate infill and rehabilitation. The code is attracting developers and investors to New Jersey's mature communities by making projects in older buildings simpler and less expensive.

The Rehabilitation Subcode has facilitated the preservation of the historic character of this building in the Mill Hill Section of Trenton, New Jersey.

Berit Seiple Osworth, New Jersey Department of Community Affairs

All the other statutes presented in this chapter are land development regulations promulgated by local governments. Other types of regulations, however, also have dramatic impacts on the ability to implement New Urbanist objectives. Prominent among these are construction codes. Construction codes aren't often associated with policy implementation, but from New Jersey comes the first example of a state-led attempt to deliberately use a building code to stimulate infill development. Specifically, the Rehabilitation Code is intended to increase the adaptive reuse of urban buildings, control suburban sprawl, and encourage urban reinvestment. The code also addresses historic buildings with special requirements and provisions applicable to structures that meet the standards for historic buildings established by the U.S. Secretary of the Interior.

New Jersey's Rehabilitation Code is the first building code written expressly for existing buildings. Not surprisingly, this landmark effort was made in a state where more than half of the housing stock was built before 1959. The code, which was adopted in 1998, controls all matters concerning the repair, renovation, alteration, reconstruction, change of use, and addition to all building sand structures, and is applicable to all existing structures in the state. The New Jersey Division of Codes and standards estimates that the subcode reduces the cost of old-building renovation between 10 and 40 percent.

The Rehab Code was developed by the New Jersey Department of Community Affairs (DCA) with guidance from a 30-member committee composed of code and fire officials, architects, historic preservationists, advocates for people with disabilities, representatives of affordable housing, and government officials. The committee met over a period of two years.

The State of Maryland also has adopted a rehabilitation code with the same objectives. See: www.op.state.md.us/smartgrowth/smartcode/smartcode00.htm.

	REPAIR	RENOVATION	ALTERATION	RECONSTRUCTION	CHANGE OF USE	ADDITION
	6.4	6.5	6.6	6.7	6.31	6.32
Certain Materials Prohibited/Required 6.4–6.7	✔	✔	✔	✔	✔d	✔e
Not Diminish Structural Strength, System Capacity 6.4–6.7	✔	✔	✔	✔	✔d	✔e
Materials & Methods 6.8		✔	✔	✔	✔d	✔e
New Building Elements— Comply with UCC 6.9			✔	✔	✔d	✔e
Basic Requirements a 6.10–6.30			c	✔	To be determined according to Hazard Index d	✔e
Supplemental Requirements b				✔	✔d	✔e
Special Change of Use Requirements					To be determined according to Hazard Index	

NOTES:

a Apply only to the work area of the project.

b Apply to the work area of the project but may apply beyond.

c Cannot reduce the level of compliance with the Basic Requirements.

d Any other work voluntarily undertaken in connection with a change of use must comply with the requirements of the appropriate category.

e Work in the existing building must comply with the requirements of the appropriate category. The addition itself must comply with the subcodes for new construction and cannot extend the size of the building beyond the limits allowed by this subcode.

Source: Information Kit, New Jersey Rehabilitation Code, New Jersey Dept. of Community Affairs.

In contrast to a conventional approach, New Jersey's rehabilitation subcode requirements are based upon the type of work being done rather than on the extent of the work (the sole exception is in some cases when reconstruction projects are large in terms of floor area). Six categories of work are defined and requirements applied as shown above.

Key Features of the Regulations

Rehabilitation subcode requirements are based on the type of work being done rather than on the cost of the work. Previously, buildings whose use was changed and buildings receiving rehabilitation costing more than 50 percent of the replacement cost of the building were required to comply with all the provisions of the Uniform Construction Code for new buildings. The new code classifies work into six categories, with separate sections establishing the requirements for each. The categories are:

1. repair;
2. renovation;
3. alteration;
4. reconstruction;
5. change of use; and
6. additions.

Meeting Regulatory Objectives

Stimulating infill and rehabilitation activity. Stimulating rehabilitation activity is the overarching objective of the code. The code's provisions are based on four principles:

1. The Rehab Code rejects the conventional code enforcement idea that requires additional work when a building owner undertakes an improvement project.
2. No building should be less safe after a project than it was before.
3. Owners should be able to predict scope and cost of projects before beginning.
4. The Rehab Code's requirements should not discourage the incremental improvement of buildings.

This building on Broad Street in downtown Newark, New Jersey, has undergone rehabilitation work under the Subcode.

ORLANDO, FLORIDA, SOUTHEAST SECTOR PLAN

Source document: Southeast Orlando Sector Plan Development Guidelines and Standards, Chapter 68, City of Orlando Land Development Code, adopted May 10, 1999

Code authors: Calthorpe Associates

Staff contact: Paul Lewis, Growth Management Staff, City of Orlando Planning Department, paul.lewis@cityoforlando.net

Web site: www.cityoforlando.net/planning/deptpage/sesp/sesp.htm

Techniques illustrated:

- New Urbanist principles are being applied in planning for a major urban expansion area that includes unique environmental features.

- The standards use incentives to promote development consistent with the regulations.

- The plan creates a full hierarchy of places from Town Center to Village and Neighborhood Centers, residential neighborhoods, and airport support districts.

- A permanently protected ecological system is part of the plan.

With a 2000 population of almost 186,000 and a projected 2010 population of close to 212,000, Orlando is planning for growth. In its comprehensive planning and growth management activities, the city has identified Southeast Orlando as a future growth center, with the Orlando International Airport as the primary economic and employment generator. Plans for the area envision a buildout population of approximately 65,000.

The Southeast Sector Plan area cover 19,300 acres situated between two regionally significant natural systems—the Econlockhatchee River and Boggy Creek. The site is in two major drainage basins, and natural features include a system of lakes and small water bodies, wetlands, and a great diversity of plants and wildlife, many of which are protected by the Orlando's Growth Management Plan and federal and state regulations.

For-sale rowhouses in NorthLake Park at Lake Nona, a traditional neighborhood development adjacent to a planned mixed-use neighborhood center. The two-car garages are accessed via rear alleys.

The Southeast Orlando Sector Plan requires a mix of housing type. The NorthLake Park apartments feature "tuck-under" apartments with parking accessed from the rear.

Key Features of the Regulations

The development regulations for Southeast Orlando are a product of a detailed planning effort begun in 1995 by the city in partnership with area public agencies and property owners. The result of that effort is a plan and associated regulations intended to create a community, rather than a suburb, including a full hierarchy of places ranging from a unique downtown to village and neighborhood centers, residential areas, and employment areas focused on the airport. The Development Guidelines and Standards were adopted as an illustrated document including planning principles, guidelines, and standards. The standards themselves have been incorporated into the City of Orlando Land Development Code as Chapter 68.

The regulations apply to all parts of the Southeast Sector area within Orlando (12,000 of the almost 20,000 total acres). The way in which the regulatory provisions are applied varies with different land-use designations. For all development in planned town centers, village centers, urban transit centers, neighborhood centers, and residential centers, the provisions of the code are mandatory. A graphic matrix summarizes key provisions for these districts. In areas with other land-use designations, however, the plan allows development under conventional regulations in certain circumstances.

The regulations are somewhat general in a number of respects. Detailed planning is to be conducted by project proponents, who must receive approval for a Specific Parcel Master Plan that will regulate the development and use of their property following approval by the city council. Approval requires consistency with the Southeast Area regulations.

Benefits to developers are described in the following provisions:

> Consistent with the Southeast Orlando Development Plan Agreement, when proposed development is consistent with the Southeast Orlando Sector Plan, participating property owners/developers shall be entitled to the following benefits:
>
> 1. Waiver of fees for Growth Management Plan amendments arising from the Southeast Orlando Sector Plan with processing of any necessary amendments by the City.

2. Waiver of fees for zoning amendments arising from the Southeast Orlando Sector Plan with processing of any necessary amendments by the City.

3. Waiver of fees for PD review and specific parcel Master Plans.

4. Waiver of City subdivision platting fees for a period of 5 years from the initial Master Plan approval of individual development parcels.

5. Local environmental permitting, if such permitting is instituted at the City's sole discretion.

6. Expedited permitting as a result of above.

The following base development incentives shall be available where Traditional Design standards, as outlined in the Southeast Orlando Sector Plan, are used:

1. Utilization of smaller Traditional Design street widths.

2. Increased densities and greater opportunities for mixed use development alternatives.

3. Transportation Impact Fee Schedule revised to reflect shorter average trip lengths, greater interconnectively, higher pedestrian accessibility and better jobs/housing balance.

The Southeast Orlando Plan contains four types of mixed-use centers. Each must be composed of a minimum mix of block types that are regulated by specific development standards.

	Town Center **Urban Transit Center**	**Village Center** **Urban Transit Center**	**Neighborhood Center**	**Residential Center**
Mixed Use Blocks	15% to 40% of Center	15% to 40% of Center	12% to 25% of Center	12% to 25% of Center
Mix of Uses* *30-80% retail, cinema, or hotel required each block, 20-70% other.	Retail, Services, Restaurants, Office, Cinema, Grocery, Hotel, Residential, Civic, Park/Plaza	Grocery, Local-Serving Retail and Services, Restaurants, Gas Stations, Professional Offices, Residential, Civic, Park/Plaza	Neighborhood Retail up to 100,000 sq.ft., Grocery up to 50,000 sq.ft., Services, Restaurant, Office, Civic, Hotel, Residential, Park/Plaza	Small Retail, Market (no more than 10,000 sq.ft.) Restaurant/Cafe, Services, Civic, Residential, Park/Plaza
Maximum Block Size	7 acres	7 acres	N/A	4 acres
Minimum FAR	FAR: 0.4	FAR: 0.3	N/A	N/A
Minimum Frontage	65% of each street	65% of each street	N/A	65% of each street
Parking Ratio	3 spaces: 1,000 sf	3 spaces: 1,000 sf	AC-N Standards Apply	3 spaces: 1,000 sf
Building Height	2 to 10 story	1 to 3 story	1 to 3 story	1 to 3 story
Commercial Blocks	0% to 30% of Center	0% to 30% of Center	0% to 13% of Center	0% to 13% of Center
Allowable Uses	Office, Retail (10% Max)	Office, Retail (10% Max)	Office	Office
Maximum Block Size	7 acres	4 acres	N/A	3 acres
Minimum FAR	FAR: 0.4	FAR: 0.3	N/A	N/A
Minimum Frontage	65% of each street	65% of each street	N/A	65% of each street
Parking Ratio	3 spaces: 1,000 sf	3 spaces: 1,000 sf	AC-N Standards Apply	3 spaces: 1,000 sf
Building Height	2 to 10 story	1 to 3 story	1 to 2 story	1 to 2 story
Residential Blocks	30% to 75% of Center	40% to 75% of Center	52% to 78% of Center	52% to 78% of Center
Allowable Uses	Apartments, Condos, Townhomes, Duplexes, Small Lot Single Family	Apartments, Condos, Townhomes, Duplexes, Small Lot Single Family	Apartments, Condos, Townhomes, Duplexes, Small Lot Single Family	Apartments, Condos, Townhomes, Duplexes, Small Lot Single Family
Maximum Block Size	3 acres	3 acres	N/A	3 acres
Density Range	7 to 50 du/acre	7 to 25 du/acre	7 to 25 du/acre	7 to 25 du/acre
Minimum Frontage	65% of each street	60% of each street	N/A	60% of each street
Parking Ratio	1.5 spaces/unit	1.5 spaces/unit	1.5 spaces/unit	1.5 spaces/unit
Building Height	2 to 5 story	1 to 3 story	1 to 3 story	1 to 3 story
Civic Blocks	10% of Center	10% of Center	10% of Center	10% of Center
Allowable Uses	Parks, Recreation, Civic, Day Care	Parks, Recreation, Civic, Day Care	Parks, Recreation, Civic, Day Care	Parks, Recreation, Civic, Day Care
Maximum Block Size	3 acres	3 acres	N/A	3 acres

Source: Southeast Orlando Sector Plan, Illustrated Guidebook, Land Use Guidelines and Standards, p. 25.)

Meeting Regulatory Objectives

Allowing a variety of uses. The standards require that the various types of centers each include four types of blocks: mixed use, commercial, residential, and civic. The mixed-use blocks are required to have a specified percentage of retail, cinema, or hotel.

Fostering mixed residential density and housing type. Housing mix is required, with allowable types specified along with a maximum density expressed as units per acre or a range of densities in some cases.

Building the public realm: Streetscape and civic life. Public spaces and civic uses are prominently addressed in the guidelines. Civic Blocks are required to comprise 10 percent of the acreage of town center areas. Allowable uses are parks, recreation, civic, and day care.

Conserving the natural environment. A Primary Conservation Network (PCN) is identified on the Master Plan Map to preserve natural areas and wetlands important for wildlife habitat and drainage for the plan area. The regulations include additional guidelines to supplement those promulgated by regional, state, and local environmental agencies. The PCN is defined as a land-use category as follows:

> 2. Primary Conservation Network. The Primary Conservation Network (PCN) establishes an interconnected open space system that protects wetland communities and habitat for numerous common and protected wildlife species while allowing passive recreation uses such as pedestrian and bike trails.

SAN ANTONIO, TEXAS, UNIFIED DEVELOPMENT CODE

Source document:	Municipal Code Chapter 35, adopted May 2001
Code authors:	Freilich, Leitner and Carlisle; HNTB-LDR International; and Ximenes and Associates
City contact:	Bill Telford, Planning Department; Gene Dawson, Pape Engineers
Web site:	www.sanantonio.gov/dsd/udc
Techniques illustrated:	• This citywide code incorporates mandatory New Urbanist provisions as well as offering parallel regulations through several use patterns, including those for traditional neighborhood development, transit-oriented development, and commercial retrofit.
	• The zoning and subdivision regulations are integrated into a Unified Development Code.
	• Mixed residential districts with different unit types are permitted as of right.

San Antonio, originally settled under the principles of the Laws of the Indies, approved a new Master Plan in 1997. The plan, which is a policy document without a land-use map, led to a full revision of the city's zoning ordinance. The new regulations, organized into a Unified Development Code (UDC), collect most of the city's land-use development regulations in a single volume. (The UDC does not include the building code or regulations governing development in the Edwards Aquifer Recharge Zoning District (ERZD) or the city's sign regulations, all of which are codified in other parts of the city code.) The code uses a number of New Urbanist tools, including the option of development under standards for traditional neighborhood districts (TNDs) and transit-oriented developments (TODs). Additional features include the use of transfer of development rights (TDRs) and the establishment for the first time of required set asides for park and open space land.

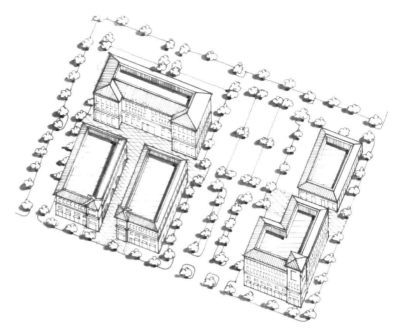

Source: San Antonio Unified development Code, Art. 2: Use Patterns, 35-204: Commercial Center, p. 2-25.

Key Features of the Regulations

Because it is comprehensive in scope, the UDC is close to 900 pages in length. Only a very small number of the code's provisions can be highlighted here. The code incorporates New Urbanist principles into base districts, such as three mixed residential districts in which single-family detached units, accessory dwellings, townhouses, and two- and three-family dwellings are all permitted uses. The UDC also creates an Infill Development Zone as a special district, which can be mapped at the behest of San Antonio's Department of Housing and Neighborhood services or an applicant, and which provides incentives for infill projects.

An innovative feature of the UDC is the use of conventional zoning districts in an unconventional way. In addition to the use lists typical of conventional ordinances, the UDC permits as of right a number of "use patterns" in specified districts. The use patterns are six forms of development that may be selected at the option of the applicant. They are coded and illustrated at the beginning of the UDC, consolidating the various development standards in a concise, user-friendly format. The Use Patterns recognize conventional subdivisions, which are the predominant form of development in many cities. As an alternative, however, the Use Patterns establish the following six development alternatives:

1. Conservation Development

2. Commercial Center Development

3. Office or Institutional Campus Development

4. Commercial Retrofit Development

5. Traditional Neighborhood Development (TND)

6. Transit-Oriented Development (TOD), but only in a transit district, which is a special district

For each of these, Article 2 of the Code establishes use, dimensional, and design regulations as well as permitting procedures. The alternative use patterns all have some unique design provisions and share others with regulations elsewhere in the ordinance. All of the alternative use patterns incorporate New Urbanist principles. The most dramatic departure from

COMMERCIAL CENTER DEVELOPMENT POLICY, SAN ANTONIO, TEXAS

A Commercial Center provides shopping, service and employment opportunities within walking or driving distance of residential areas. The Center is spatially defined and concentrated in a nodal pattern, as opposed to conventional strip shopping centers. Commercial Centers feature urban design guidelines such as zero setbacks and streetscapes with windows and entryways. The Commercial Center Use Pattern implements the following policies of the Master Plan:

• Urban Design, Policy 1a: Based on a comprehensive land use plan, encourage more intensive development in and near neighborhood centers with less intensive development between neighborhood centers, and implement these changes through zoning.

• Urban Design, Policy 1e: Permit zero setbacks for commercial developments.

The provisions of this section are designed to permit commercial centers in a wider variety of districts and situations, subject to strict design standards that prohibit strip development and encourage walkable streetscapes. Freestanding commercial uses that do not meet the standards of this section shall be located in the "C" Commercial zoning district.

conventional local practice is the "Commercial Center" Use Pattern. The commercial center provisions allow a zero front setback and require that all commercial center buildings "shall have their principal entrance opening to a street, square, plaza or sidewalk" (Section 35-204(4)(A)). In order to stimulate pedestrian activity, the regulations require that new commercial buildings along major roads have a minimum of 50 percent of ground-floor frontage dedicated to retail use. A Commercial Center is permitted as of right in every residential zoning district with a minimum lot size of less than 20,000 square feet, and as a specific use (in Texas, a "specific use" is the equivalent of a conditional use or special use) in all other residential districts, with the location dependent upon adjoining street classifications.

A significant benefit of the San Antonio approach is that in zoning districts where the TND use pattern is allowed, a TND development consistent with the provisions of the ordinance can be approved administratively with a combined Subdivision Plan and Master Site Plan.

Meeting Regulatory Objectives

Allowing a variety of uses. In TNDs, the code specifies minimum land allocation for parks and open space, civic uses, retail or service uses, multifamily, and single-family uses, thus requiring a mix of both uses and housing types. The Commercial Retrofit use pattern permits the introduction of new uses on retail-only "greyfield" sites.

In the code's C-1, C-2, C-3, and Downtown base districts, a range of residential and commercial uses are permitted as of right.

Fostering mixed residential density and housing type. In addition to the optional use patterns for TOD and TND, the code establishes three residential mixed-use districts, which allow detached, attached, and multifamily dwellings as of right. Accessory dwellings are a permitted use in residential-mixed-use and all single-family districts. Vertical mixed uses such as mixed-use buildings and live-work units are permitted in many commercial and mixed-use zoning districts.

Stimulate infill and rehabilitation. The district provides incentives for infill projects including:

1. easing setback provisions;

2. exempting infill projects from many of the code's standards, including the traffic impact analyses; and

3. exempting infill projects from the code's minimum parking requirements.

Creating compact, walkable downtowns and neighborhoods served by public transit. Many of the code's provisions implement this objective. The TOD use pattern is established specifically for transit station areas. The UDC establishes caps on the amount of parking for all uses and zoning districts. Specific street design guidelines are established for TND and Conservation Subdivisions, and street widths were narrowed for conventional subdivisions as well. A connectivity ratio is established for streets to provide multiples routes for drivers and pedestrians.

Building the public realm. The TND use pattern requires that 2 percent of TND land be dedicated to civic uses, and that prominent sites be reserved for civic buildings, hotels, or office buildings. The Park and Open Space standards are design oriented. Rather than simply require that a minimum amount of parks be set aside and maintained, design templates are provided for different categories of civic spaces, including greenways, squares, and plazas.

Requiring quality design reflecting built and natural environments. The Infill Development Zone includes urban design standards requiring (and defining):

• compatibility in massing;

• spacing between buildings;

• proportion of windows, bays, and doorways; and

• other features.

Protecting natural environments and conserving resources. UDC provisions include establishment of a TDR system, with sending zones including critical areas and agricultural areas, as well as special provisions for flood hazard zones. The parks and open space standards encourage connectivity with adjoining parks. Parking lot shading standards are included, and the preservation of existing and native vegetation is credited toward landscaping requirements. As of May 2004, the city was in the process of updating its tree preservation ordinance.

HUNTERSVILLE, NORTH CAROLINA, ZONING ORDINANCE

Source document:	Zoning Ordinance, adopted November 19, 1996; as amended through July 16, 2001
Code authors:	Town planning staff
Website:	www.Huntersville.org/planning/ordinances.htm
Techniques illustrated:	• Mandatory New Urbanist provisions are integrated in an ordinance that replaced conventional zoning.
	• Transit-oriented development (TOD) standards apply to future transit station areas.
	• The ordinance uses graphics extensively to illustrate its provisions. For instance, seven building and lot types, graphic standards, and brief accompanying text explain building placement/parking/vehicular access, encroachment/pedestrian access, permitted height and uses, and architectural standards.

Vermillion was the first project approved under the Huntersville Code as a traditional neighborhood development (TND) district.

In Huntersville, 12 miles north of Charlotte, North Carolina, a completely new zoning code is one part of the town's response to rapid growth and intense development pressure. The town learned the hard way that the wrong zoning code leads to the wrong kind of development. Now, development in new growth and intensification areas, including those around a planned light rail line, will be designed and built according to the mandatory provisions of the new code, which emphasizes traditional urbanism and quality design.

Huntersville is one of a cluster of three towns—Cornelius and Davidson are the others—that have collectively been working to combat sprawl, preserve rural lands, and integrate land use with transit investments. Together, they comprise approximately 100 square miles of Mecklenburg County. All have adopted New Urbanist codes. While all three codes are based on common principles, the regulations themselves vary in approach and specific provisions.

Key Features of the Regulations

The zoning code adopted by Huntersville in 1996 replaced the town's code in full. The provisions, which emphasize the principles of traditional town planning, TOD, and quality urban design, are mandatory. All new development must conform to:

1. *district regulations* (Article 3), specifying purpose, uses permitted conditionally and as of right, general requirements, and permitted building and lot types;

2. *building and lot regulations* (Article 4), form-based provisions including graphics and text that describe, for seven building types, standards for site planning and architecture (see example below);

3. *street regulations* (Article 5), specifying eight street types and describing a variety of street plan types; and

4. *off-street parking, landscaping and open space, general provisions, and sign regulations.*

Most of the districts have been mapped under the town's initiative. The TND district, by contrast, has been mapped only at the request of applicants with properties meeting size and locational criteria. The TOD districts have not been mapped because light rail is not yet serving Huntersville.

Parks and Squares are two of the six types of urban open spaces defined in the Huntersville Ordinance. Each is graphically illustrated and contains standards, including minimum site size, permitted materials, typology, and other design standards.

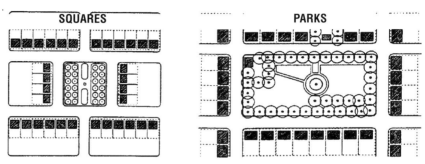

Source: Huntersville Zoning Ordinance, art. 7: Landscaping and Open Space, p. 140.

Meeting Regulatory Objectives

Allowing a variety of uses. The code allows a wide range of commercial and residential uses in many of the zoning districts. Statements of intent establish the expectation that a mix of uses will be created in neighborhood centers, the town center, and TNDs and TOD. The shopfront building type accommodates small-scale vertical mixed use. For TNDs, a master plan must be submitted showing the location of lots dedicated to different uses as well as illustrating other features.

Fostering mixed residential density and housing type. The Neighborhood Residential District provides for residential infill development and permits multifamily and single-family housing as of right in apartments and attached and detached houses. In major subdivisions, the total number of units in multifamily and mixed-use buildings may be up to 30 percent of the total number of units in the project as of right. A mixture of housing types and prices is called for in TND districts. There is no requirement for a specified mix.

Requiring quality design. The Neighborhood Residential District provides for residential infill. Buildings are required to "respect the general spacing of structures, building mass and scale, and street frontage relationships of existing buildings." Architectural standards require that "development shall generally employ building types that are sympathetic to the historic architectural vocabulary of the area in their massing and external materials." These apply to all building types except highway commercial.

Creating compact, walkable downtowns and neighborhoods. Site and street design requirements in articles three and five of the code contribute

LOT TYPE / URBAN WORKPLACE

**BUILDING PLACEMENT/
PARKING/VEHICLE ACCESS**

**ENCROACHMENT/PEDESTRIAN ACCESS
TO BUILDING**

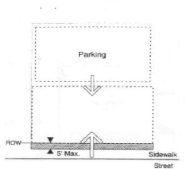

BUILDING TYPE / URBAN WORKPLACE

PERMITTED HEIGHT AND USES

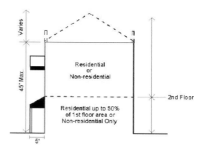

Source: Huntersville Zoning Ordinance, art. 4: Building and Lot Types, pp. 82-83.

These graphics illustrate the standards for "shopfront" buildings, one of seven building types allowed in the Huntersville code. Each zoning district specifies those building and lot types that are permitted, as well as listing uses permitted as of right and conditionally.

to meeting this objective. The Neighborhood Center District (NC) permits as of right detached and attached housing and civic, mixed-use, shopfront, and workplace buildings. The intent of the district is to provide for "the location of shops, services, small workplaces, civic and residential buildings central to a neighborhood or grouping of neighborhoods and within walking distance of dwellings." New neighborhood centers are shown on the town's Land Development Plan. By contrast, the Town Center District (TC) provides for revitalization, reuse, and infill in Huntersville's traditional center. Standards applying to the district allow for the higher overall development intensity that will be required to support a future rail transit center.

Building the public realm. The code's provisions are intended to define public space through placement and design of buildings as well as through street design. Article 4, Building and Lot Type, addresses building placement, parking and vehicle access, encroachment, and pedestrian access. Street regulations are established in Article 5 and apply to streets not maintained by the state. The street regulations prescribe that "As the most prevalent public spaces in Huntersville, streets should be spatially defined by buildings." This principle is illustrated in the ordinance, as are specifications for eight different street types. All streets other than rural roads, lanes, and alleys are required to interconnect, to be bordered by sidewalks on both sides, be lined with street trees, be public, and be the focus of buildings.

Protecting natural environments and conserving resources. Two overlay districts are established to protect the quality of public water supplies in the Mountain Island Lake and Lake Norman watersheds. These require higher standards in the critical areas where there is the greatest risk of water-quality degradation. The code limits impervious services, requires specified vegetative buffers, and offers a higher density development option (requiring special permits) when engineering controls are used to manage storm water runoff.

The Open Space district provides for "development of compact neighborhoods and rural compounds that set aside significant natural vistas and landscape features (rural heritage features) for permanent conservation." Density is regulated on a sliding scale with allowable densities rising as the extent of preserved open space rises.

Source: Huntersville Zoning Ordinance, art. 3: zoning districts, 3.2.1.e) farmhouse cluster, p.12.

The Open Space District encourages the development of compact neighborhoods that set aside significant rural heritage features for permanent conservation. The farmhouse cluster is one of six development typologies allowed in the district.

PETALUMA, CALIFORNIA

Source document: Central Petaluma Specific Plan and SmartCode, adopted June 2, 2003

Code authors: Fisher & Hall Urban Design with assistance from: Crawford Multari & Clark Associates, Sargent Town Planning, Patrick Siegman, Nelson\Nygaard Consulting, Pete Musty, CharretteCenter.com

City contact: Mike Moore, Community Development Director, mmoore@ci.petaluma.ca.us

Website: http://ci.petaluma.ca.us/; http://ci.petaluma.ca.us/cdd/cpsp.html

Techniques illustrated:

- Mandatory New Urbanist provisions are integrated into a specific plan and zoning ordinance as a form-based SmartCode to replace conventional zoning for a 400-acre infill site.

- The code incorporates three new mixed-use zones based upon the rural-to-urban Transect: T-4 General Urban, T-5 Urban Center, and T-6 Urban Core.

- Block perimeter, lot coverage, building placement, building heights (minimum and maximum), parking location, and street types are all coded based upon historical urban fabric, walkability, and community preferences.

- Parking standards that eliminate on-site parking requirements are included. A "Sunset Clause" establishes a new policy effective January 1, 2008, that eliminates all minimum parking requirements after that date. On-site parking is to be oriented to the backs of the buildings and the interiors of the blocks.

- The code is extensively illustrated.

In 1972, Petaluma, California, became the first city in the United States to impose systematic growth controls within its boundaries. In 2003, Petaluma became the first city in the United States to adopt a SmartCode for a major infill area. The code was adopted with the objective of telling developers exactly what the community wants new development to look like in this infill area that includes historic neighborhoods, aging shopping centers, industrial and commercial redevelopment areas, and vacant industrial sites.

Through a process of community workshops and committee discussion, Petaluma developed a clear vision of their preferred future for Central Petaluma. That vision is one of pedestrian-oriented public streets, plazas, squares, and riverfront walks, lined with mixed-use, pedestrian-oriented buildings. The scale and general character of new development is based on elements of Petaluma's built heritage: the multistory mixed-use shopfront buildings of the historic Downtown, the iconic agricultural buildings, and the rich variety of streets, riverfront wharfs, plazas, and parks of the city's historic center.

The Central Petaluma SmartCode provides a system for ensuring that the design of the public realm and the design of private buildings are rigorously coordinated and focused on the pedestrian experience. It defines what is essentially a "kit of parts," providing instructions for building an urban district based on the preferences of the community. The focus of this technique is on the scale and character of the parts and how they connect to each other. The focus is *not* on the architectural styling of the parts, for which standards are flexible.

The SmartCode defines an agreement between the community and private property owners. The community commits itself to building and maintaining high-quality, pedestrian-oriented streets, public parking facilities, squares, plazas, and riverwalks, while the property and business owners commit themselves to building high-quality buildings that face the public realm with facades scaled to the pedestrian.

PETALUMA, CALIFORNIA, URBAN STANDARDS

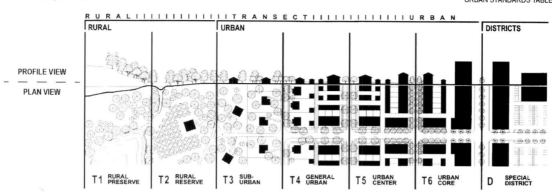

RURAL | | | | | | | | | | | | | T R A N S E C T | | | | | | | | | | | | U R B A N

PROFILE VIEW

PLAN VIEW

T1 RURAL PRESERVE	T2 RURAL RESERVE	T3 SUB-URBAN	T4 GENERAL URBAN	T5 URBAN CENTER	T6 URBAN CORE	D SPECIAL DISTRICT
BLOCK & LOT DESIGN						
Block perimeter				2,000 lf. max. 2,400 lf. max. for blocks with internal structured parking	1,700 lf. max. 2,000 lf. max. for blocks with internal structure parking	1,700 lf. max. 2,000 lf. max for blocks with internal structure parking	Refer to Section 4.20
Lot Area				4,000 sq. ft. avg.	2,000 sq. ft. min.	2,000 sq. ft. min.	
LOT COVERAGE				60% max.	80% max.	100% max.	
BUILDING PLACEMENT							
Edge Yard				permitted	prohibited	prohibited	Refer to Section 4.20
Side Yard				permitted	permitted	prohibited	
Rear Yard				permitted	permitted	permitted	
Court Yard				permitted	permitted	permitted	
BUILDING SETBACK							
Front				0 ft. min. 15 ft. max.	0 ft. min. 10 ft. max.	0 ft. min. 5 ft. max.	Refer to Section 4.20
Side				5 ft. min. 30 ft. max.	0 ft. min. 10 ft. max.	0 ft. min. 10 ft. max.	
Rear (Applies to lots not served by alleys)				20 ft. min. to principal building 5 ft. min. to outbuilding	20 ft. min. to principal building 5 ft. min. to outbuilding	20 ft. min. to principal building 5 ft. min. to outbuilding	
Alley (Measured from centerline of Alley)				15 ft. min.	15 ft. min.	15 ft. min.	
FRONTAGE TYPE (See Section 4.40 and Section 5.10)							
Common Yard				permitted	prohibited	prohibited	Refer to Section 4.20
Porch and Fence				permitted	prohibited	prohibited	
Terrace or Light Court				permitted	permitted	prohibited	
Forecourt				permitted	permitted	permitted	
Stoop				permitted	permitted	permitted	
Shopfront and Awning				permitted	permitted	permitted	
Gallery				prohibited	permitted	permitted	
Arcade				prohibited	permitted	permitted	
DENSITY				25 units per acre max.	60 units per acre max.	60 units per acre max.	60 units per acre max.
% BUILDING FRONTAGE REQ. (See Section 5.10)							
Principal Frontage				50% min.	75% min.	90% min.	Refer to Section 4.20
Secondary Frontage				30% min.	35% min.	50% min.	
BUILDING HEIGHT							
Principal Building				3 stories max.	2 stories min. 4 stories max.	3 stories min. 6 stories max.	Refer to Section 4.20
Outbuilding				2 stories max.	2 stories max.	not applicable	
PARKING LOCATION (See Section 6)							
1st Layer				prohibited	prohibited	prohibited	Refer to Section 4.20
2nd Layer				prohibited	conditionally prohibited	conditionally prohibited	
3rd Layer				permitted	permitted	permitted	
PARKING REQUIREMENTS							
Residential (Including Live/Work)				1 space per unit	1 space per unit	1 space per unit	Refer to Section 4.20
Lodging				1 space per room	1 space per room	1 space per room	
All other uses				1 space/300 gross sq. ft. of building area	1 space/300 gross sq. ft. of building area	1 space/300 gross sq. ft. of building area	
BUILDING FUNCTION (See Section 3)							Refer to Section 4.20
CIVIC SPACES (See Section 4.50)							
Nature Park				permitted at waterfront	permitted at waterfront	permitted at waterfront	Refer to Section 4.20
Green				permitted	permitted	permitted	
Square				permitted	permitted	permitted	
Plaza				prohibited	permitted	permitted	
Playground				permitted	permitted	permitted	
Public Open Space				permitted	permitted	permitted	

Key Features of the Regulations

The Central Petaluma Specific Plan and SmartCode replaced the city's zoning ordinance within the project area. The provisions, which emphasize the principles of traditional town planning and transit-oriented development, are mandatory. The SmartCode is intended to ensure that all new buildings are contextually appropriate with each other and Petaluma's character, and that the area evolves into new, mixed-use neighborhoods with the following characteristics:

- The size of neighborhoods reflects a five-minute walking distance from edge to center (center meaning a railroad transit stop or the existing downtown).
- The mixture of land uses includes shops, workplaces, residences, and civic buildings in proximity.
- A variety of thoroughfares serve the needs of the pedestrian, the cyclist, and the automobile equitably.
- Public open spaces provide places for informal social activity and recreation.
- Building frontages define the public space of each street.

Meeting Regulatory Objectives

Allowing a variety of uses. The three new transect zones created in the project area all allow for varying degrees of mixed use. T-4, General Urban, and T-5, Urban Center, permit home occupations, live-work units, and residential in mixed-use buildings as of right. T-6, Urban Core, permits mixed-use buildings as of right.

Fostering mixed residential density and housing types. The three new zones provide for various types of residential infill development. T-4, General Urban, and T-5, Urban Center, permit multifamily and single-family housing as of right. T-6, Urban Core, permits residential in a mixed-use building as of right.

Stimulate infill and rehabilitation activity. The SmartCode stimulates infill in a number of ways. First, it significantly streamlines the approval process for new projects by requiring applicants to get approval only from the design review board. In the past, applicants often had to get approvals from the planning commission and city council as well. Also, strong community participation in the preparation of the SmartCode potentially reduces the number of project appeals.

The SmartCode stimulates rehabilitation activity by eliminating requirements for on-site parking, thereby allowing existing/historic buildings to changes uses to those, such as cafes and restaurants, which in the past would not have been allowed due to the on-site parking requirements. Rehabilitation activity is also stimulated because properties in the Smart-Code area are now zoned to more intense and valuable uses, thereby increasing the potential value and opportunities for new uses in nearby existing/historic buildings.

Develop contextual design standards ensuring that new development responds to the traditional architectural styles of the city or region. Architectural guidelines in the SmartCode describe existing patterns and recommend design approaches. These guidelines support architecture that preserves and strengthens the much-prized character of the existing town and its distinct neighborhoods, while creating a compatible character in newly developed areas.

Create compact, walkable centers and neighborhoods served by public transit. The Central Petaluma area contains tremendous opportunities to cultivate viable alternative modes of transportation that will be supported

PETALUMA, CALIFORNIA, BUILDING FRONTAGE STANDARDS

CENTRAL PETALUMA SMART CODE   SECTION 4.40
PETALUMA, CALIFORNIA   FRONTAGE TYPES

4.40 - Frontage Types

The street facing facades of each proposed building shall be designed as one of the building frontage types allowed by Section 4.10 (Urban Standards Table). Allowed frontage types shall be designed in compliance with the following standards.

Common Yard: a frontage wherein the façade is set back substantially from the frontage line. The front yard created remains unfenced and is visually continuous in landscaping with adjacent yards, supporting a common rural landscape. Common Yards are suitable along higher speed thoroughfares, as the deep setback provides a buffer.

Porch and Fence: a frontage wherein the façade is set back from the frontage line with an attached porch encroaching. The porch should be within a conversational distance of the sidewalk. A fence at the frontage line maintains the demarcation of the yard. Porches shall be no less than 8 feet wide.

Terrace or Light Court: a frontage wherein the façade is set back from the frontage line by an elevated garden or terrace, or a fenced, sunken light court. This type buffers residential use from urban sidewalks, removing the private yard from public encroachment. The terrace is suitable for outdoor dining.

Forecourt: a frontage wherein a portion of the façade is close to the frontage line while a substantial portion of it is set back. The forecourt created is suitable for gardens and drop-offs. This type should be allocated sparingly in conjunction with other frontage types. Trees within the forecourts may overhand the sidewalks.

Stoop: a frontage wherein the façade is aligned close to the frontage line with the lower story elevated from the sidewalk sufficient to secure privacy for the windows. The access is usually an exterior stair and landing. This type is recommended for ground-floor residential uses.

Shopfront and Awning: a frontage wherein the façade is aligned close to the frontage line with the building entrance at sidewalk grade. This type is conventional for retail use with a substantial glazing on the sidewalk level, and an awning placed so as to overlap the sidewalk to the maximum possible.

Gallery: a frontage wherein the façade is aligned close to the frontage line with an attached cantilevered shed or a lightweight colonnade overlapping the sidewalk. This type is appropriate for retail use. The Gallery shall be no less than 10 feet wide and overlap the whole width of the sidewalk to within 2 feet of the curb.

Arcade: a frontage wherein the façade is above a colonnade that overlaps the sidewalk, while the sidewalk level remains at the frontage line. This type is appropriate for retail use. The arcade shall be no less than 12 feet wide and overlap the whole width of the sidewalk to within 2 feet of the curb.

13

by the SmartCode's permitted densities of 25 to 60 units to the acre. The area is traversed by a railroad and the river. The railroad, which is currently used for freight, has the potential for passenger service. The river is navigable and currently is used primarily for freight, but also has the potential for transit service. The plan calls for renovation of the historic Petaluma Depot for passenger rail service along the proposed Sonoma-Marin line and to serve as the new hub for the city's bus transit center. With increased congestion along U.S. 101, it may also become feasible in the future to provide ferry service from Petaluma to San Francisco and other ferry ports in the Bay area.

Enhance streetscapes and civic life. All streets in the SmartCode are custom-designed to support pedestrian and civic life. Wide sidewalks, narrower streets, pedestrian-scaled site furnishings, and minimum building heights all result in a street proportion and character that supports pedestrian activity. A central feature of this plan is the river as the focus of civic life in this area.

Shape metropolitan regions with public space, farmland and natural areas. Petaluma is a city that is set apart from other communities by a buffer of agricultural lands and undeveloped open space. Within the city, the Petaluma River is perhaps the city's greatest open space. Comprising nearly 40 acres within the SmartCode project area, the river establishes an opening within the urban fabric with vistas framed by bridges and shoreline. With the complex and lively new development coded for in the SmartCode, Petaluma will continue to benefit from its high value natural areas as well as the complex urban fabric and public spaces that continue to be shaped by them.

COLUMBUS, OHIO, TRADITIONAL NEIGHBORHOOD DEVELOPMENT

Source document: Traditional Neighborhood Development Article, Article II, Columbus Zoning Code, adopted May 21, 2001

Code authors: City staff and Duany Plater-Zyberk

City contact: Reza Reyazi, Long-Range Planning Division, rereyazi@columbus.gov

Website: www.columbusinfobase.org/eleclib/elechome.htm.

Techniques illustrated:
- The zoning code incorporates a parallel traditional neighborhood development (TND) code.
- Transect zones are the organizing principle for TND zones.
- A graphic matrix identifies the street and civic space types allowed in each of the four different TND zoning districts.

TRANSECT

Source: Columbus Zoning Code, Art II: Traditional Neighborhood Article, Chapter 3320.013: Transect, p.2.

The base districts of the Traditional Neighborhood Development Article are based on the concept of the Transect, organizing the variation between suburban and urban in four idealized zones.

Columbus, the largest city in Ohio, began considering the adoption of neo-traditional development standards in its 1993 Comprehensive Plan. With the leadership of a member of the city council, an implementing ordinance for Traditional Neighborhood Development (TND) was adopted in May 2001. Unlike a number of other cities, where parallel TND ordinances have languished without being applied, Columbus passed its first rezoning to the TND district only two months after adoption of the regulations. The first project to be approved under the regulations was Upper Albany.

Key Features of the Regulations

Columbus' Traditional Neighborhood Development Article presents a regulatory alternative that may be requested by a property owner through a rezoning application. The rezoning application must include a site plan indicating which of the four TND zoning districts established by the Article are to be applied, and where.

The districts, which parallel the urban-to-rural transect zones, are:

1. *Neighborhood Edge:* the least dense, primarily residential part of a community. It consists principally of single-family, detached houses with outbuildings permitted. Civic spaces are parks and greens.

2. *Neighborhood General:* primarily residential part of a community, typically the largest area within the pedestrian shed. It consists of single-family, both attached and detached, houses with one outbuilding permitted on each lot. Civic spaces are parks, greens, and squares.

3. *Neighborhood Center:* the denser, fully mixed-use part of a community. It consists primarily of attached buildings and apartment houses without outbuildings. The parking, which is substantial, must be accessed by rear alley and located behind the front façade of the building. The civic spaces are squares and greens.

4. *Town Center:* the densest business, cultural, and entertainment concentration of the community. Buildings are attached and often tall, situated on a wide range of lot sizes. All uses not considered noxious are permitted within the buildings.

A distinguishing feature of the Columbus regulations is that areas as small as two acres may be zoned for TND. The four different districts use mandatory regulations that result in a greater mix of district types for larger projects (e.g., projects larger than 100 acres must have at least 10 percent of the project area contained in each of three TND districts) and prohibit projects of any size from allocating more than 50 percent of the project area to the Neighborhood Edge District.

Another feature of the regulations is the use of a point system as part of the administrative review process that follows rezoning approval. Applicants must submit a regulating plan, which is reviewed in relation to a checklist requiring conformance with all mandatory elements of the code and with at least 50 percent of the points awarded for inclusion of elements classified by the code as "desirable."

Meeting Regulatory Objectives

Allowing a variety of uses. The code describes the neighborhood and town center districts as the mixed-use parts of the community. While the specific provisions of the code do not mandate how the mix is to be achieved, the rezoning application process requires that the applicant demonstrate the application's consistency with the purpose and intent of the article.

Fostering mixed residential density and housing type. As with the mix of uses, a general principle rather than a specific formula for mixed housing type is included in the code. It states that "A variety of housing stock serves a range of incomes and age groups and includes backyard apartments, apartments above shops and residential units adjacent to work places." The applicant must demonstrate that this principle is satisfied by the project. Depending on the TND District, several type of housing are allowed and promoted.

Stimulating infill and rehabilitation activity. The Columbus Article differs from many others in that it may be applied to sites as small as two acres. This opens the door for the city's TND provisions to be used on infill sites.

Creating compact, walkable downtowns and neighborhoods. One intent of the ordinance is to promote "transit-supportive" neighborhoods, and the streetscape has to be designed to provide a balance between the interests of

---

PURPOSE STATEMENT IN THE COLUMBUS, OHIO, TRADITIONAL NEIGHBORHOOD DEVELOPMENT PROVISIONS

The purpose of this Article is to encourage the development of transit-supportive mixed-use neighborhoods that foster pedestrian activity and a sense of community. It recognizes that many activities of living should occur within easy walking distance, giving independence to those who do not drive. It also recognizes the importance of linkages to the broader community and the importance of public transit as a viable alternative to the automobile by providing appropriate densities and land uses within walking distance of the transit stop. . . . It is the intent of this Article to provide for a development pattern that can reduce trip demand and infrastructure costs, and to create more viable communities, by adapting the land development principles that guided our country's first settlements, towns, cities and suburbs.

Source: Columbus Zoning Code, Art. II: Traditional Neighborhood Article, Chapter 3320.01: Purpose, p.1.

all its users. Many of the regulatory provisions address that objective through the fundamentals of New Urbanist design: connected thoroughfares, width of walkways, implementation of bicycle trails, commercial uses on first floor, and more.

Protecting natural environments and conserving resources. Chapter 3329.01 of the ordinance specifically addresses natural and historic resources. Not all of the provisions are mandatory. Developments, however, must apply at least 50 percent of the provisions.

Building the public realm. The design of the public realm is fully integrated in the regulations, which address in detail mandatory and desired elements of the thoroughfare network, civic spaces and civic buildings, and private buildings, for which frontage types are described and illustrated.

The Permitted Thoroughfare Types by District table shows which of 19 thoroughfare types are permitted in the four TND zoning districts. Thoroughfare Standards tables are included for each type. These graphic standards are accompanied by text provisions that specify mandatory elements for thoroughfares, such as network connectivity, and desired elements, such as landscaped medians in all but neighborhood edge districts. Each of these elements is assigned a maximum score to be used in the point system that is part of the City's review process.

	NEIGHBORHOOD EDGE (NE)	NEIGHBORHOOD GENERAL (NG)	NEIGHBORHOOD CENTER (NC)	TOWN CENTER (TC)
MAXIMUM BLOCK LENGTH	1000 FT MAX.	900 FT. MAX.	700 FT. MAX.	600 FT. MAX.
THOROUGHFARE TYPES				
PS-0-8			▪	▪
PT-0-8	▪	▪	▪	
LA-16-12	▪	▪	▪	
AL-22-22			▪	▪
AL-86-60				
CL-42-22	▪	▪		
ST-52-26 S	▪	▪	▪	
T-48-22	▪	▪	▪	
CO-54-26		▪	▪	▪
CO-60-32		▪	▪	▪
BV-76-40	▪	▪	▪	▪
BV-120-60				▪
BV-90-60			▪	▪
CS-62-36			▪	▪
CS-112-88			▪	▪
CS-88-64			▪	▪
CS-73-49				
CS-75-51			▪	▪

Source: Columbus Zoning Code, Art. II: Traditional Neighborhood Article, Chapter 3320.15: Thoroughfares.

ARLINGTON COUNTY, VIRGINIA, COLUMBIA PIKE SPECIAL DISTRICT

Source document:	Columbia Pike Special Revitalization District Form Based Code, Section 20 (Appendix A) of the Arlington County Zoning Ordinance—"CP-FBC", adopted February 25, 2003
Code authors:	Geoffrey Ferrell Associates, Dover, Kohl & Partners Town Planning
County contact:	Richard Tucker, Columbia Pike Planner, Rtucker@arlingtonva.us
Website:	http://www.co.arlington.va.us/forums/columbia/
Techniques illustrated:	• The zoning code incorporates a parallel Columbia Pike form-based code (CP-FBC) for a 3.5-mile revitalization district corridor with multiple parcels and owners.
	• Provisions employ incentives, particularly streamlined administrative approval process and economic development tools.
	• The Regulating Plan is complemented with graphic building envelope standards (e.g., placement, massing, functional elements) keyed to street frontage.

Arlington, Virginia, an urban county "inside the Beltway" directly across the Potomac River from Washington, D.C., has seen explosive development along the Metro corridors for the past 30 years (and witnessed suburban sprawl in outlying Fairfax, Loudon, and Prince William counties) while Columbia Pike, the Main Street for the southern portion of the county, has languished. The Pike, a historic thoroughfare from the Pentagon to the County Line (the original southwestern border of the District of Columbia), saw virtually no development throughout the boom years of Northern Virginia. County leadership wanted to encourage redevelopment but, at the same time, direct and control the type of development. The aim was to create a mixed-use, pedestrian environment (which was virtually non-existent) while planning for future light rail or bus rapid transit (BRT) along the corridor, retaining the ethnic/eclectic diversity of the community, and maintaining small, locally owned businesses and existing affordable housing.

The Columbia Pike Revitalization Organization (CPRO) and county staff embarked on a 150-meeting, two-year educational and visioning process, meeting with the many neighborhood, business, and property owner groups and condo associations and ultimately producing a community vision. The County Board endorsed a plan in March 2002 that targeted specific areas for redevelopment and began introducing New Urbanist concepts. They concurrently recognized the need to implement tools to move the plan from concept to reality. A week-long public charrette led to a more specific master plan for the corridor as well as a form-based code to amend the zoning ordinance for the designated revitalization districts.

One infill live-work project designed under the code broke ground in 2003. (The developer waited for the code to be passed because the project would not have been allowed under the county's existing zoning ordinance.) Several other property owners/developers were in discussion with the county and the Revitalization Organization at the time of the code's passage.

Key Features of the Regulations

The CP-FBC is optional, a strategy chosen by the county in order to avoid any potential "takings" issues. It has no direct impact on existing buildings and uses. If they choose to do so, all property owners still have the right to redevelop using their existing underlying zoning and by-right options, or to proceed through the county's alternative site plan approval process.

The CP-FBC approval process is streamlined. For all properties smaller than 40,000 square feet, development under the CP-FBC is a by-right option with approvals handled administratively by county staff in 30 days or less. For properties larger than 40,000 square feet, the projects can proceed under an expedited special exception use permit process, as long as the development follows the form-based code. Approval under special exception is expected within 60 days. In both cases, approval is based on a set of standards intended to eliminate the sometimes unpredictable outcomes of discretionary review.

The code is organized around a series of street frontages—"main street," "local street", "avenue," and "neighborhood street"—with building envelope standards established for each. In addition there are architectural standards—essentially a "dress code"—that are fairly loose (the community desired an eclectic style, rather than limiting new development to any particular aesthetic), primarily addressing fenestration, materials, doors, roofs, and walls and fences.

Columbia Pike Revitalization
Building Envelope Standards
Main-Street Sites

Height

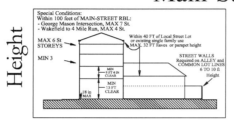

Special Conditions:
Within 100 feet of MAIN-STREET RBL:
- George Mason Intersection, MAX 7 St.
- Wakefield to 4 Mile Run, MAX 4 St.

MAX 6 St STOREYS
MIN 3

Within 40 FT of Local Street Lot or existing single family use MAX 32 FT Eaves or parapet height

STREET WALLS Required on ALLEY and COMMON LOT LINES 6 TO 10 ft Height

MIN 5 FT 4 IN CLEAR
MIN 15 FT CLEAR
18 in MAX

The building shall be between 3 and 6 STOREYS in height, except where otherwise noted here or on the REGULATING PLAN.

Any parking structure w/in the block shall not exceed the eave height of any building (built after 2002) w/in 50 feet.

Any unbuilt ALLEY and/or COMMON LOT LINE frontage shall have a STREET WALL built along it, between 6 feet and 10 feet in height.

The GROUND STOREY floor elevation shall be between 0 inches and 18 inches above the fronting sidewalk elevation.

No less than 60% of the ground floor shall have at least 15 feet clear height. No less than 80% of the upper STOREYS shall each have at least 9 feet 4 inches clear height.

Siting

(RBL)   REQUIRED BUILDING LINE
ALLEY or INTERIOR LOT LINE
MIN 75% BLDG ALONG REQUIRED BLDG. LINE
MINIMUM OPEN CONTIGUOUS LOT AREA 15%
25 FT Setback where no ALLEY EXISTS
REQUIRED BLDG LINE   REQUIRED BUILDING LINE (RBL)

The STREET facade shall be *Built-To* the REQUIRED BUILDING LINE (RBL) within 30 feet of any BUILDING CORNER, and *Built-To* not less than 75% of the overall RBL. There are no required side lot line setbacks unless shared with an existing single family house where a 10ft setback is required.

Any unbuilt RBL and or COMMON LOT LINE shall have a STREET WALL along it, between 6 feet and 10 feet in height.

On sites with no ALLEY access there shall be a 25 foot setback from the rear lot line.

Garage/parking entrances shall be no closer than 50 feet from any BUILDING CORNER or 100 feet from any BLOCK CORNER (except where otherwise designated on the REGULATING PLAN).

These illustrations and text are included in the code, which aims to establish a traditional main street pattern of ground-floor retail with residential in upper stories.

Elements

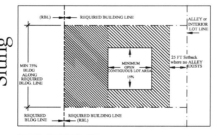

UPPER FACADES FENESTRATION MAX 70% MIN 30%
STREET FACADE FENESTRATION MAX 90% MIN 60%

The GROUND FLOOR facade shall have between 60% and 90% FENESTRATION (measured between 2 and 10 feet above the fronting sidewalk). Awnings and overhangs are encouraged (except where otherwise designated on the REGULATING PLAN).

Upper STOREY facades shall have between 30% and 70% FENESTRATION (measured for each STOREY between 3 and 9 feet above the finshed floor).

ARCADES are permitted on some streets, if designed and constructed in contiguous STREET FRONTAGES of at least 200 feet (or any complete RBL fronting a SQUARE or CIVIC GREEN), consult the DEFINITIONS.

Uses

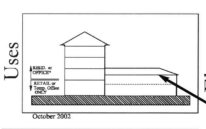

RESID. or OFFICE*
RETAIL or Temp. Office ONLY

October 2002

The ground floor shall house only retail or temporary office uses (also lobby and access for upper storey uses).

*Upper storey uses may be either: (along X Avenue) residential, or (along Y Road), residential, office or lodging.

There shall be functioning entry door(s) along the STREET facade at intervals not greater than 70 feet.

The garage (parking for vehicles autos, trailers, boats, etc.) shall be setback at least 20 feet from any STREET FRONTAGE (except for basement garages). Except where otherwise designated on the REGULATING PLAN.

NON-RETAIL
RETAIL or OFFICE ONLY

The GROUND FLOOR shall house only retail or office uses (also lobby and access for upper storey uses).

Retail uses are not permitted on the upper storeys (except those of less than 900 Sq Ft and/or second storeys as an extension of the GROUND STOREY use and with direct Columbia Pike frontage). Second storey restaurants do not violate this rule.

There shall be functioning entry door(s) along the STREET facade at intervals not greater than 60 feet.

Any garage (parking for vehicles autos, trailers, boats, etc.) shall be set back at least 25 feet from any RBL (except for basement garages). Except where otherwise designated on the REGULATING PLAN.

Source: Columbia Pike Special Revitalization District Form Based Code (courtesy of Geoffrey Ferrell Associates).

Allowing a variety of uses to create vitality and bring many activities of daily living within walking distance of homes. All of the CP-FBC frontage designations, with the exception of neighborhood streets, allow for a mix of uses, with shopfront buildings being required on the main street areas, with the expressed intent of requiring ground-floor retail, although there is some flexibility provided with respect to upper-floor uses.

Fostering mixed residential density and housing types. A mixture of housing types are allowed on different street types—from apartments, to townhouses and live-work units, to detached single family—regulated by placement on the lot and mass, rather than density. In addition, the code expressly allows accessory units.

Stimulating infill and rehabilitation activity. The CP-FBC was created to stimulate and then shape infill development. If property owners choose to redevelop under the new, more prescriptive code, they gain development potential relative to by-right zoning. Use of the code also opens the door to the county economic development fund. The fund was created specifically to spur appropriate growth on Columbia Pike. In addition, small properties have been relieved of on-site parking requirements, providing owners with greater flexibility/ability to redevelop or rehabilitate their properties.

Developing contextual design standards that ensure new development responds to the traditional architectural styles of the city or region. The CP-FBC specifically addresses design and scale through the Regulating Plan, Building Envelope Standards, and Architectural Standards in a number of ways:

- The maximum floor-plate of new construction is limited.

- Individual large building façades are required to be broken up to read as separate buildings.

- Minimum and maximum heights are prescribed (based on stories rather than feet).

- Functioning street entries at maximum average distances are required.

- Parking lots and structures at the street frontage are prohibited.

- Interior block vehicular access through the creation of an alley system is required.

- Streets reconnect through some megablocks.

- There are incentives for protection and inclusion of "historic" structures and facades in new development

Each of these features will contribute to the overall design and scale of Columbia Pike, creating the desired pedestrian-oriented main street and village center environment.

Creating compact, walkable centers and neighborhoods served by public transit. The Columbia Pike corridor is already a major transit (bus) route, but the plan also incorporates the anticipated evolution to streetcar, light rail, or bus rapid transit. The plan designates four "centers"—each to have at least one future transit stop—where more dense mixed-use redevelopment is encouraged through the CP-FBC. The departments of public works and planning worked together with the consultant team to establish minimum street standards for the future transit-way—street widths, sidewalks, tree pits, medians—while maintaining pedestrian-oriented centers throughout the long-term redevelopment of the Pike.

This sketch illustrates the design concept underlying applicable provisions of the code, showing one way that buildout under the code's standards could create the desired level of urbanism and public amenity.

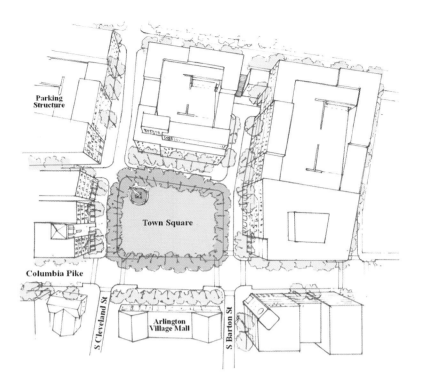

Enhancing streetscapes and civic life. The Regulating Plan establishes build-to lines for each street in the revitalization district and the code establishes building envelope standards, which jointly form the desired street space. The CP-FBC also details the design of that space through the specific requirement and placement of street trees, streetlights, and shopfront buildings, among other features. In addition, the county has designated public spaces—greens and squares—in each of the "centers," and the code specifically regulates the building that will define those spaces.

THE HERCULES, CALIFORNIA, CENTRAL PLAN

Source document: Regulating Code for the Central Hercules Plan, Adopted July 2001

Code authors: Dover, Kohl and Partners

City contact: Steve Lawton, Community Development Director, slawton@ci.hercules.ca.us

Website: www.ci.hercules.ca.us; www.hercules-plan.org

Techniques illustrated:
- Regulatory Plan includes planning policies, development regulations, and illustrations.
- The city puts strong emphasis on development and design standards accompanied by conventionally formatted use table.
- Development under the code is ruled by a hierarchy of street types, each of which specifies street standards, building placement, and building volume.
- The plan and regulations use illustrations extensively.

Hercules is a suburban community in western Contra Costa County in the San Francisco Bay Area. The Regulating Code applies to approximately 425 acres of waterfront property that include the former site of the Hercules Powder Company, one of the world's largest dynamite manufacturing plants. In late 1999, the Hercules Planning Commission embarked on establishing a unified design for a set of major projects that would establish the design character of Hercules for the next generation. The entire planning and regulatory effort was inspired by the community's desire to attract the "right kind" of development, to create a town center that would take advantage of a stunning waterfront site, and to distinguish Hercules from its suburban neighbors. The city initiated a major planning and urban design initiative that resulted in the 2000 adoption of the Central Hercules Plan. A year later, the city adopted the Regulating Code for the Plan.

Key Features of the Regulations

Development under the code is regulated by a hierarchy of street types. For each street type, the code regulates street standards, building placement, and building volume. The code also includes a set of architectural regulations with the primary goal of "achieving authenticity of design elements." These regulations address building walls, opacity and facades, columns, arches, piers, railings and balustrades, windows, skylights and doors, roofs and gutters, garden walls, fences and hedges, and signs. Special regulations apply to large footprint buildings, which may be approved only by conditional use permit.

The plan's provisions are mandatory on most area properties, yet, on some, property owners may elect to develop under the new code or the preexisting General Plan designations.

Meeting Regulatory Objectives

Allowing a variety of uses. An extensive use list identifies for each of the area's four districts allowed uses, permitted uses (with a conditional use permit), and prohibited uses. For example, the Regulating Code states that

> The City expects a mix of allowed uses to occur in all neighborhoods and blocks. The City will require a mix of uses within buildings along the Four Lane Avenue. The City will require neither particular uses nor a particular distribution of uses. The City will require the integration of residential and commercial uses.

In the foreground are post-tensioned slab foundations for new development in the Hercules Waterfront District. In the background are the historic company townhouses (once part of the site of one of the world's largest dynamite factories) and a recently constructed small residential subdivision.

REGULATING PLAN

One of the primary tools used for implementing New Urbanism on large sites or multiple-property areas is the "Regulating Plan." This is a series of plan documents and text provisions that lay out a detailed plan for a given geographic area that may or may not involve multiple landowners. The Regulating Plan covers the essential elements of New Urbanism: the street, alley, and block structure; requirements for build-to lines, yards, and building massing; the horizontal and vertical mixing of uses; the placement of street trees and other natural elements; parking locations and requirements; and the location of squares, greens, plazas, parks, and civic buildings (which may be public or private). It typically includes some architectural standards, although these are usually more at the level of architectural syntax than detailed design. Regulating Plans are usually quite prescriptive in their requirements for urbanism but flexible in their use standards. They are highly illustrated with plans, charts, diagrams, and drawings, carefully annotated to make their meaning clear.

Regulating Plans integrate a number of elements that typically are not addressed in a single ordinance: use, dimensions, parking, and landscape provisions commonly found in zoning; streetscape provisions usually found in both subdivision regulations and municipal public works programs; recommended lot divisions that typically result from the subdivision approval process; and various design standards that can come in separate ordinances or as part of historic districts, special design regulations, design guidelines, or zoning. A Regulating Plan can be prepared at a variety of levels of detail, depending upon the size of the area being regulated, the degree of prescriptiveness the community wishes to impose, and budgetary constraints.

These instructions appear on page 2 of the Regulating Code to instruct the user about the various new provisions that apply to properties within the Central Hercules area:

How to Use the Regulating Code

1 Determine whether your use is permitted in the Central Hercules Plan area.

2 Determine whether your site falls within the Waterfront District, Central Quarter, Civic Center/ Hospitality Corridor, or Hilltown.

3 Determine which Street Type your lot fronts. . . . Review Chapter II for provisions about the Street Type that correspond to the lot.

4 Review the Use Table (Chapter III) and the General Provisions (Chapter VI) which apply throughout the Central Hercules Plan area.

5 Review the Projecting Façade Elements and Architectural Regulations (Chapter IV) which contain specific rules for Buildings.

Source: Regulating Code for the Central Hercules Plan, Chapter I: Intent & Use of this Code.

In addition to those provisions, which apply to the four-lane avenue, Main Street is described as "lined with mixed-use shopfront buildings."

Fostering mixed residential density and housing type. Neither residential density nor lot size is regulated by the code, which instead establishes requirements for building placement and volume. Housing type is likewise not explicitly regulated. Single- and multi-family (attached and detached) housing, secondary or carriage units, and live-work units are all allowed as of right in three of the four Central Hercules districts.

Sources: Photo by Steve Lawton; drawing from the Herculers Waterfront District Plan by David Sargent; composite by Toby Zallman.

This residential street maintains 28-foot-wide (curb to curb) streets and is clearly consistent with the diagram from the Regulatory Plan.

Alleys provide access to rear garages in the developing Hercules Waterfront District.

Building the public realm. Site, building, and street design parameters are established through requirements for building placement and volume, standards for projecting facade elements, and architectural regulations. Each of these is associated with a specific street type from a palette that is the basis for regulation under the code. Civic buildings are not subject to build-to line or building frontage requirements, but their design is subject to planning commission review.

THE SAINT PAUL, MINNESOTA, URBAN VILLAGE CODE

Source document: Urban Village Code, April 2004

Code authors: URS Corporation

City contact: Allan Torstenson, allan.torstenson@ci.stpaul.mn.us

Website: www.stpaul.gov/depts./ped

Techniques illustrated:

- The regulations for major urban infill sites are incorporated into a traditional zoning district format.

- New development is integrated into its surroundings by establishing mixed-use and proximity requirements that can be satisfied by on- or off-site activities.

- Many housing types are allowed as of right in traditional neighborhood development (TND) districts.

In its 1999 comprehensive plan, Saint Paul confronted the need for new land-use and transportation models to accommodate future growth. Using the principles of New Urbanism to support additional growth in the central city is one key strategy. The plan summary notes that:

> The "Traditional Neighborhood Design" and "New Urbanism" movements represent recognition of the value of Saint Paul's neighborhoods in contrast to typical suburban development. New Urbanist practices provide some direction for maintaining and enhancing the strengths of our existing neighborhoods.

The Comprehensive Plan's General Policy 5 sets forth the concept of neighborhoods as urban villages, noting that:

> Opportunities to live, work and shop in close proximity will reinforce the urban village characteristics of Saint Paul neighborhoods. Improvements and new developments should contribute to a high quality, visually inviting, pedestrian-friendly environment. Land Use and Housing chapter policies support application of urban village principles in neighborhood planning and development.

The city's urban village zoning project is one of the ways Saint Paul is implementing this policy.

Key Features of the Regulations

Saint Paul's new regulations introduce three traditional neighborhood districts.

- TN-1 is a transitional zone between higher-intensity commercial districts and residential neighborhoods, and may replace two existing districts.

- TN-2 is a general mixed-use district mapped on some but not all commercial districts.

- TN-3 is intended for large redevelopment sites, which will constitute the city's new urban villages.

The new districts include design guidelines that apply to various degrees in each of the three, with broadest applicability in the TN-3 urban village areas. Sites developed under the TN-3 regulations will almost always require that a master plan be prepared by the city or by a developer. The broader urban village code program also includes additional zoning and subdivision ordinance revisions to eliminate several existing zoning districts as well as barriers to traditional neighborhood development.

APPLICABILITY OF TND GUIDELINES, SAINT PAUL, MINNESOTA

TND Guidelines	TN-1	TN-2	TN-3
Diversity: More than one use/building type on any 2 contiguous blocks			■
Change of use at rear/side lot line			■
Similar facing buildings		■	■
Transitions to lower-density neighborhoods		■	■
Block length (400–660 feet)		■	■
Compatible alteration or remodeling of traditional buildings	■	■	■
Use established building façade line	■	■	■
Buildings anchor the corner	■	■	■
Front yard landscaping	■	■	■
Building façade continuity		■	■
Façade articulation—base, middle and top	■	■	■
Vertical articulation of façade	■	■	■
Building height—treatment of 1-story buildings	■	■	
Visible, identifiable entries	■	■	■
Definition of residential entries	■	■	■
Door and window openings—minimum and character	■	■	■
Materials—primary and accent	■	■	■
Screening of equipment and service areas		■	■
Interconnected street and alley network; parking both sides		■	■
Parking underground or to rear, limited side parking	■	■	■
Surface parking >30 feet from corner	■	■	■
Residential garage location	■	■	■
Parking lot lighting		■	■
Locate entrances for convenient access to transit stops	■	■	■
Street trees—provide in street r.o.w.	■	■	■
Sidewalks	■	■	■

Source: St Paul Urban Village Code draft, April 2002, TND Design Guidelines and related Ordinance Revisions, p.19.

Three Traditional Neighborhood Districts are introduced in the draft of St Paul's regulations. This matrix shows what design elements are addressed in each of the three districts.

Some or all of the urban village sites will be rezoned under a focused planning effort known as a 40-acre study. New districts will be applied only as a result of 40-acre studies by the city or by a petition for rezoning by property owners. The new districts will expand the menu of land-use controls available to neighborhoods and developers for study and future use.

Meeting Regulatory Objectives

Allowing a variety of uses. A wide range of residential, institutional, civic, office, and commercial uses are permitted as of right in each of the districts, with the mix being permissive in TN-1 and TN-2 zones. A mix of uses is required in TN-3 districts and must be composed of at least two land-use categories as well as centrally located public open space.

Fostering mixed residential density and housing type. All three TNDs allow many attached housing types as of right. Only the TN-3 allows single-family detached dwellings as well as a variety of multifamily types. Congregate living facilities, including community residential facilities serving up to 16 residents, are also permitted as of right.

The TN-3 district requires a mix of unit types in projects with more than 50 units, as well as requiring that at least half of all units are multifamily, in mixed-use buildings, or attached single-family units.

Stimulate infill and rehabilitation activity. "Stimulating infill and rehabilitation" is a basic objective of the urban village zoning program and is addressed through many provisions of the proposed code.

Require quality design. Site plan review is required in all TNDs. Development guidelines to be used include the requirement that "new development . . . relate to the design of adjacent traditional buildings, where these are present, in scale and character." (See also table on applicability of TND guidelines on page 75.)

Creating compact, walkable downtowns and neighborhoods. This objective is met with many of the code's provisions. Some of these relate to parking. Surface parking is restricted to the rear or side of lots and is allowed as a principle use only when it is shared among multiple businesses. The code establishes the intensity needed for compact neighborhoods in part by instituting minimum standards for density and commercial FAR in TN-2 and TN-3 districts. Parking requirements are reduced along "transit streets" in the TN-1 and TN-2 districts (streets with peak-hour transit headways of 10 minutes or less). The TN-3 district allows on-street parking to partially satisfy parking requirements.

Building the public realm. This objective is met with many of the code and guideline provisions. The table on page 75 lists features addressed in the guidelines.

THE SKANEATELES, NEW YORK, VILLAGE CENTER

Source document: Village of Skaneateles Zoning Law, Local Law No. 7 of the year 1996 (zoning law amendments to the Local Law No. 2 of 1975)

Code author: Joel Russell, Woodlea Associates

Website: www.townofskaneateles.com/index.shtml

Techniques illustrated:
• The regulations maintain traditional village character.
• The regulations define elements that contribute to the traditional Main Street pattern of the village center and codifies them to maintain and extend the historic pattern.

The Village of Skaneateles, in Central New York State's Onondaga County, has a historic downtown whose character is protected and reinforced through the provisions of the Village Zoning Law. The provisions of the Downtown (D) district promote the maintenance, preservation, restoration, and economic use of the historic structures of the center of the village and the gradual extension of the village center in the same pattern.

Key Features of the Regulations

The Downtown district provides standards applying to the private and public realms, since the character of the downtown is shaped by both pub-

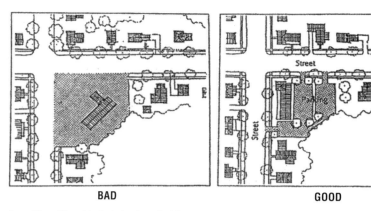

BAD   **GOOD**

Source: Village of Skaneateles Zoning law, Appendix A, Section 15-44, d: General Standards for the Downtown Districts - Corner Lots, p. 9.

These illustrations show how the basic elements of good pedestrian street design are graphically explained, often by comparing a bad example vs. a good example. This type of small drawing is a main component of this zoning law.

lic improvements and privately owned land and structures. The Downtown Design Standards have three parts:

1. General standards for the Downtown District, containing provisions mostly directed towards the streetscape
2. Specific standards for lots with party wall buildings
3. Specific standards for lots with detached buildings

All are mandatory provisions illustrated by pictures and drawings, and often followed by a short explanation of the reasons of the rule. The provisions encourage the mix of use, without providing any specific requirements, and contain no architectural style standards as they are focused primarily on the definition of type of streetscape and buildings. The result is a graphic-based code, showing in very clear and simple language the image that the village intends to maintain, restore, and expand.

Meeting Regulatory Objectives

Allowing a variety of uses. The code is focused more on the type of buildings and their configuration than on their function. Therefore, it permits the combination of uses without requiring a particular mix. Apartments are allowed on upper floors of mixed-use buildings.

Fostering mixed residential density and housing type. The code allows as permitted uses one-family, two-family, and townhouse dwellings in the Downtown district, as well as up to three apartment units on upper floors of mixed-use buildings. There are no requirements for a certain level of mix, but the building typology (party wall and detached) implies several housing types and a mixed residential density.

Requiring quality design reflecting built and natural environment. Considering that one of the intents of the code is to maintain and extend the pattern of the village center, the major part of the provisions for the downtown district aim to ensure the compatibility with the context. They require compatibility in height, massing, type of roofs, building alignment and layout, building materials, proportions of windows and bays, and other features.

Creating compact, walkable downtowns and neighborhoods. Many of the provisions of the code promote the "pedestrian-oriented character of the Village" (art. IV, sect. 15-110) or aim to "maintain a pleasant and safe pedestrian environment." That objective is implemented through the regulation of various aspects of the public space: sidewalks, building frontage, curb radii, windows and entrances facing the street, commercial uses on the first floor, and on- and off-street parking.

> ### THE SKANEATELES CODE LANGUAGE GOVERNING QUALITY DESIGN
>
> The streetscape and the relationship of the private buildings to the public realm is one of the main concern of the downtown district regulations.
>
> > Buildings should have a well-defined front façade with entrances facing the street. Building should be aligned so that the dominant lines of their facades parallel the line of the street and create a continuous edge. Departures from this regular pattern should be allowed only to terminate important vistas along streets or sidewalks or to act as focal points for public spaces.
>
> *Source:* Village of Skaneateles Zoning law, Appendix A, Section 15-44, d: General Standards for the Downtown Districts - Building layout, p. 2.

Building the public realm. "Building the public realm" is one of the main objectives of the code, which states:

> Although zoning normally applies only to private and semi public uses, these standards assume that public-private partnership and cooperation will be an integral element of the development within the D district. (Section 15-44, d, 1)

Therefore, most of the general provisions of the Village Center District describe the streetscape and the public spaces in relation to the buildings.

Protecting natural environments and conserving resources. One overlay district is established to protect the ecological and scenic character of Skaneateles Creek from development that would adversely affect its resource value and its potential use as a pedestrian trail corridor.

PASADENA, CALIFORNIA, CITY OF GARDENS

Source document:	Multifamily Zoning Ordinance, adopted February 1989
Code authors:	Solomon E.T.C., in collaboration with Christopher Alexander and Phoebe Wall
City contact:	John Poindexter, Planning Manager, jpoindexter@ci.pasadena.ca.us
Website:	www.ci.pasadena.ca.us/planning/deptorg/dhp/gardens.asp
Techniques illustrated:	• The ordinance provisions are based on detailed study of historic architecture and landscape design. • These provisions resulted from an early New Urbanist effort highly focused on a small number of high-priority local objectives.

Pasadena's renowned gardens and courtyard housing provided the inspiration for a zoning approach first codified by the city in February 1989. Known as the City of Gardens Ordinance, Pasadena's multifamily standards apply to projects in multifamily residential districts (RM) and to residential projects in the limited commercial (CL) and commercial office (CO) districts.

The intent of the ordinance is to continue to permit high-density development while incorporating design features typical of Pasadena's historic pattern. The regulations reflect the design tradition of viewing the private garden as a coherent and useful space that plays a role in shaping development as is as important as building volume and parking layout.

This approach, requiring new development to be more in scale and character with existing neighborhoods, was developed partly in response to residential development that has been unsympathetic to the city's garden character.

PASADENA'S COMMITMENT TO GARDENS AS AN INTEGRAL ELEMENT OF MULTIFAMLY HOUSING

The Pasadena ordinance confirms in its garden standards how gardens contribute to the public realm of the multifamily district of Pasadena.

> More than any other single factor it is the presence of gardens and landscaped areas that creates the ambience of Pasadena. Neighborhood character and quality depend on the coherence, embellishment and visibility of courts and gardens, on the size and consistency of front yards, and on the frequency and uniformity of street trees. Mandatory requirements regulating the size and configuration of yards and gardens are therefore a central feature of these provisions.

Source: Pasadena Zoning Ordinance, Chapter 17.24: RM Multifamily (City of Gardens) Residential Districts, 17.24.030: Development Standard M—Garden Standards, p. 120-58.2.

Key Features of the Regulations

The purpose statement of the ordinance makes clear that new development is to be in scale and character with existing neighborhoods. It is mostly focused on the gardens that are a signature feature of Pasadena neighborhoods, and the provisions are structured so they develop and restore a streetscape that integrates the public spaces with surrounding housing and gardens in a coherent environment

Meeting Regulatory Objectives

Reflecting both design and environmental context. This is the central objective of the ordinance. Most of the provisions reinforce the character of the multifamily zones of Pasadena. This character is attributed to certain specific features, which occur within three main categories: the character of the gardens, the character of the streets, drives and parking, and the character of the buildings. The provisions are based on a detailed study of the elements that compose these categories and tend to integrate the street and the site visually and functionally.

Building the public realm. The gardens that typify multifamily development in Pasadena are key contributors to the public realm, and the ordinance confirms their role. Gardens are required to be visible from the street, though not to be physically accessible to the public. Many additional provisions ensure the coherence and the quality of the neighborhood. These control right-of-ways, building frontages, street orientation, height of structures, garden and architectural standards, and off-street parking.

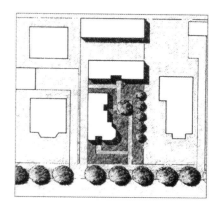

Main Garden with Adjacent House

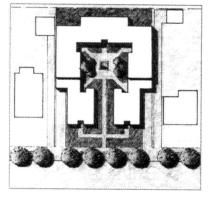

Internal Courtyard

A F T E R W O R D

Creating a Local Government System
that Promotes New Urbanism

Paul Crawford, FAICP

The successful completion and implementation of a New Urbanist code can be helped or undermined by the other components of the local system for managing development. The system includes people and the regulations and procedures with which they work.

The key components are the plan, code, administrators, and decision makers. Each is critical in the community's decisions about its future. The following sections describe how the components of the development management system other than the code should work with the code.

THE COMPREHENSIVE PLAN

The relationship between the policies of comprehensive plan and the regulations of the development code must be clear and mutually supportive. Because comprehensive plans typically have policies and a map or diagram addressing the desired types and locations of land uses, the plan should set the stage for the regulations in the code that will cover the details of how individual properties can be developed and used. This relationship is particularly important in states, such as California, that mandate consistency between plans and regulations because a code that pursues new directions for community development without a clear basis in adopted policy will be vulnerable to legal challenge. This can be problematic in a community with a comprehensive plan that calls for the segregation of land uses by type (i.e., residential, commercial, industrial, etc.) while the code is expected to provide for mixed-use neighborhoods and residential areas with a variety of housing types. If the new code is intended to fully express New Urbanist principles, the comprehensive plan should state that the "regulatory geography" in the code will define the boundaries of neighborhoods, districts, and corridors. The comprehensive plan should not continue to have a land-use diagram that appears only as a generalized version of Euclidean zoning.

PLANNING DEPARTMENT STAFF

The staff of the local planning department typically serves as the community's first contact with the people who develop property. Staff has responsibility for informing prospective developers of the community's expectations and requirements for development, explaining the applicability and effect of the local zoning regulations. The planning department is usually the source for copies of local regulations. Planning department staff are also responsible for verifying the compliance of proposed development with local regulations in the case of projects required to obtain only building permit approval. And, finally, staff has the role of evaluating the impacts and appropriateness of projects required by the code to have discretionary review, with opportunities for public input prior to final decisions by a planning commission or city council.

The community's planning department staff must be expert in the content and application of a new development code, or its goals are unlikely to be realized. Staff should, therefore, either participate in the drafting of the new code or at least have the opportunity for extensive review and discussion of its provisions while it is being drafted. Although a common characteristic of graphically oriented New Urbanist codes is their user friendliness, they look and function differently from the conventional zoning ordinances they replace. Staff should not be expected to begin the administration of a new code incorporating a substantially different approach to land-use regulation (e.g., the indirect regulation of land uses through building typologies versus explicit, comprehensive lists of permitted and conditional uses) without effective orientation and training in advance. Because staff must counsel developers, elected and appointed officials, and the public in the meaning and applicability of the new code provisions, it is important that they have the background to do so with accuracy and confidence.

Many planning department staff members may be ready to implement New Urbanism but less prepared to work collaboratively with members of the public works or transportation department. Given the emphasis New Urbanism places on the design of the public realm and on streets in particular, this collaboration is essential. It should be recognized as a challenge to bridge what is in many municipalities a deeply entrenched schism between departments.

The community's planning department staff must be expert in the content and application of a new development code, or its goals are unlikely to be realized.

APPOINTED AND ELECTED OFFICIALS

The final component of the community's development management system (other than the general public, whose role was discussed in Gianni Longo's sidebar in Chapter 2) includes the appointed and elected officials with the responsibility for making discretionary decisions about proposed projects. In many ways, the role of planning commissioners and city council members overshadows the importance of comprehensive plan policies, development code regulations, and the responsibilities of planners in the review of proposed development. This is simply because a New Urbanist code, supporting comprehensive plan policies, and complementary direction to staff will not exist without the interest and support of the decision makers who must amend the plans, adopt the codes, and manage their use. Advocates of incorporating New Urbanist principles in local development regulations must obviously, therefore, secure the support of the decision makers through education and encouragement before work on a code update is initiated.

Less obvious but equally important is the need to provide for the ongoing education and orientation of planning commissions and city councils. Individual commission and council members will change over time, so new members without background in New Urbanist principles will need information documenting their value in practice if the new members are to render development decisions that support overall community objectives. Even long-term members will benefit from periodically updated information on the experiences of the local community and other communities in the successful implementation of New Urbanist codes; providing confident leadership as a proponent of new development forms is much easier, after all, when one can point to successful examples in other communities.

Appendix A: Summary Table of New Urbanist Land Development Regulations

PART 1. MODEL CODES			
Model Codes	**Prepared By**	**Status**	**Electronic Information**
Envision Utah Model Codes and Land Use Analysis Tools for Quality Growth, and Urban Planning Tools for Quality Growth	Fregonese Calthorpe Associates, Envision Utah	Completed	www.envisionutah.org
From Policy to Reality: Model Ordinances for Sustainable Development	Minnesota Planning Environmental Quality Board	Completed September 2000	www.mnplan.state.mn.us/SDI/ordinancestoc.html
Smart Code	Duany Plater-Zyberk & Co	Published 2003	www.municode.com/smartcode/about.asp
Wisconsin: Draft of Model TND Ordinance	Brian W. Ohm, James A. LaVro, Jr., and Chuck Strawser	Approved July 28, 2001	www.wisc.edu/urpl/facultyf/ohmf/ projectf/tndord.pdf
Smart Codes for Maryland's Smart Growth: Building Rehabilitation Code	Maryland Dept. of Housing and Community Development	Adopted June 1, 2001	www.op.state.md.us/ smartgrowth/smartcode/smartcode00.htm
Washington State: Model Code Provisions: Urban Streets & Subdivisions	Washington State Community Trade and Economic Development	Completed, October 1998	www.ocd.wa.gov/info/lgd/growth/ publications/index.tpl
State of Maryland: Extensive set of model codes and guidelines	Maryland Department of Planning	Many publications complete, materials being added on an ongoing basis	www.mdp.state.md.us/planning/m&gnew.html
Model Development Code and User's Guide for Small Cities; Commercial and Mixed Use Development Code Handbook	Otak for the Oregon Transportation and Growth Management Program	Completed September 1999 and July 2001	www.lcd.state.or.us/tgm/publications.htm
Traditional Neighborhood Development: Street Design Guidelines	Institute of Transportation Engineers	Completed, October 1999	www.ite.org

Appendix A: Summary Table of New Urbanist Land Development Regulations (continued)

PART 2. STATE BUILDING CODES			
Building Codes	**Prepared By**	**Status**	**Electronic Information**
New Jersey Rehabilitation Subcode	New Jersey Department of Community Affairs	Adopted	www.state.nj.us/dca/codes
Maryland Rehabilitation Code	Maryland Department of Housing and Community Development	Adopted	www.op.state.md.us/smartgrowth/smartcode/ smartcode00.htm

Appendix A: Summary Table of New Urbanist Land Development Regulations (cont'd)

PART 3. LOCAL REGULATIONS

Local Government	Title	Prepared By	Electronic Contact
Arlington, Virginia	Columbia Pike Special Revitlization District Form-Based Code (CP-FBC); Section 20 of the Arlingrton County Zoning Oridnance	Geoffrey Ferrelll Asociates; Dover Kohl & Partners; and Arlington County staff	www.co.Arlington.va.us/forums/columbia/current; www.columbiapikepartnership.com
Atlanta, Georgia	Quality of Life Zoning Districts	City Staff	http://apps.atlantaga.gov/citydir/DPCD/Bureau_of_Planning/BOP/Zoning/Web_Pgs/zoning_districts.htm
Austin, Texas	Traditional Neighborhood District (TND) Ordinance (Austin Code of Ordinances, Vol. II, Chapter 25-3) and Criteria Manual	City Staff	www.ci.austin.tx.us/development/ldc1.htm; www.review.ci.austin.tx.us/tnd/defaulttnd.html
Belmont, North Carolina	Traditional Neighborhood District Ordinance (City of Belmont Regulating Ordinance, chapter 4-11)	Duany Plater Zyberk with City Staff	www.belmont.nc.us
Burnsville, Minnesota	Heart of the City District (Burnsville City Ordinance, Chapter 22-B) and Design Framework Manual	Dahlgren, Shardlow, and Uban Inc.; citizen steering committee; and city staff.	http:www.burnsville.org/government/plan/ord/specialuses.htm
Chattanooga, Tennessee	North Shore Commercial/Mixed-Use Zone (Ordinance 10717) and Commerical District Design Guidelines	Chattanooga-Hamilton County Regional Planning Agency	www.chattanooga.gov; www.chcrpa.org (online code not updated)
Chesapeake City, Maryland	User's Manual and Design Guidelines	City Staff and Redman & Johnson	www.chesapeakecity.com/towncoun.htm
Columbus, Ohio	Traditional Neighborhood Development (TND) Article	City Staff and Duany Plater-Zyberk	www.columbusinfobase.org/eleclib/elechome.htm

Status as of 5/15/04	Capsule Description	Condition	Area(s) Covered	Application of New Urbanist Regulations
Adopted February 2003	Directs mixed-use, pedestrian- and transit-oriented redevelopment of an urban corridor through a form-based code using regulating plan, building envelope standards, and architectural standards.	Infill, redevelopment	3.5-mile corridor, designated revitalization district	Parallel
Adopted	Four new zoning districts: neighborhood commercial, live-work, mixed residential commercial, and multifamily commercial. The provisions for these districts address the relationship of the building to the pedestrian realm, parking, and other street elements.	Infill; Reuse	Rezonings to occur following collaborative process between city and stakeholders	Mandatory, following mapping of districts
Adopted 1997	Creates a traditional neighborhood development (TND) district and an administrative process that may be requested by landowners or developers	Greenfield (areas from 40 to 250 acres)	Whole jurisdiction. Mapped at request of applicant	Parallel
Adopted August 1995	Public, civic, and shopfront design standards and provisions	Greenfield (areas from 40 to 200 acres)	Traditional neighborhood development (TND) districts	Mandatory
Adopted 1999	Establishes certain street types for the purpose of regulating building types, land uses, and setbacks.	Infill	Downtown	Mandatory
Adopted March 1998	Design guidelines (primarily oriented to improving streetscape and public space design) to guide the review of projects proposals.	Infill	Area zoned in North Shore Commercial/ Mixed-Use Zone	Mandatory
Adopted June 1999	Zoning ordinance creates a traditional neighborhood development (TND) district and a floating TND district for future implementation. Set of design guidelines supplemental to the design standards requirements.	Full range of conditions	Whole jurisdiction	Hybrid
Adopted May 2001	Creates four traditional neighborhood development (TND) districts and an administrative process that may be requested by landowners or developers	Full range of conditions (areas of two acres or more)	Whole jurisdiction. Mapped at request of applicant	Parallel

(Continued on the next page)

Appendix A: Summary Table of New Urbanist Land Development Regulations (cont'd)

PART 3. LOCAL REGULATIONS

Local Government	Title	Prepared By	Electronic Contact
Concord, North Carolina	Unified Development Ordinance	Freilich Leitner & Carlisle	http:www.ci.concord. nc.us/udo/
Cornelius, North Carolina	Land Development Code	City Staff	www.cornelius.org
Davidson, North Carolina	Planning Ordinance Overlay	Town Staff and The Lawrence Group	www.ci.davidson.nc.us
Fort Collins, Colorado	Fort Collins Land Use Code	City Staff	www.colorado.com/ftcollins/landuse/article1.htm
1. Gainesville, Florida	Land Development Code: Traditional Neighborhood Development (Article VII, Division V)	City Staff	user.gru.net/domz/tnd.htm
2. Gainesville, Florida	Land Development Code: Traditional City Overlay District and Traditional City Area Minimum Development Standards (Appendix A, Section 4)	City Staff	fws.municode.com
Gresham, Oregon	Community Development Code: Land Use Districts and Plan Districts	City Staff	www.ci.gresham.or.us/departments/cedd/dp/code.htm
Hercules, California	Regulating Code for the Central Hercules Plan	Dover-Kohl & Partners	www.ci.hercules.ca.us; www.hercules-plan.org
Hillsboro, Oregon	Zoning Ordinance: Vol II Station Community Planning Areas	City Staff	www.ci.hillsboro.or.us/Planning_Department/Default.asp
Hillsborough County, Florida	Land Development Code: Article 5, Development Options	Freilich, Leitner & Carlisle and County Staff	www.hillsboroughcounty.org/pgm/home.html

Status as of 5/15/04	Capsule Description	Condition	Area(s) Covered	Application of New Urbanist Regulations
Adopted March 2001	Creates two traditional neighborhood development (TND) districts (county-coordinated) that may be requested by landowners or developers, as well as creating a transit-oriented development (TOD) district	Full range of conditions (no minimum area for TND-infill district)	Whole jurisdiction. TND mapped at request of applicant; TOD surrounding identified transit stations.	Hybrid
Adopted October 1996	Full New Urbanist code replaced conventional zoning	Full range of conditions	Whole jurisdiction	Mandatory
Adopted June 2001	Citywide ordinance focused on restoring traditional development patterns	Full range of conditions	Whole jurisdiction	Mandatory
Adopted June 2001	Conventionally formatted citywide ordinance including mixed-use neighborhood districts with provisions requiring minimum densities, some mix of housing types, and other New Urbanist features.	Full range of conditions	Whole jurisdiction	Mandatory
Adopted June 1999	Creates a taditional neighborhood development (TND) district and an administrative process that may be requested by landowners or developers	Greenfield or major infill (areas from 16 to 200 acres)	Whole Jurisdiction. Mapped at request of applicant	Parallel
Adopted June 1998	Overlay code works in combination with underlying area zoning: the underlying districts remain in effect and are further regulated by the Traditional City standards	Infill	Traditional City overlay district	Mandatory
Adopted May 2001	The whole code is transit, mixed-use, and pedestrian oriented. It contains several sets of provisions that implement these objectives regarding the specific characteristics of each type of zone and subzone.	Full range of conditions	Whole jurisdiction	Mandatory
Adopted July 2001	Coding of building types corresponds with street type	Major reuse site	425 waterfront acres	Mandatory for most subareas, parallel for one
Adopted and Amended, April 1997	Regulation establishes 14 zoning districts for areas surrounding transit stations, distinguished by differences in emphasis on primary uses and intensity of development. Each of these, however, share a number of design and development standards	Full range of conditions	Areas surrounding transit stations	Mandatory
Updated January 31, 2001	Community design regulations including traditional neighborhood development (TND), transit-oriented development (TOD), and pedestrian-oriented development incorporated in the community development code	Greenfield and suburban retrofit	Whole jurisdiction	Optional

(Continued on the next page)

Appendix A: Summary Table of New Urbanist Land Development Regulations (cont'd)

PART 3. LOCAL REGULATIONS

Local Government	Title	Prepared By	Electronic Contact
Huntersville, North Carolina	Zoning Ordinance	Town Staff	www.huntersville.org/planning/ordinances.htm
Jupiter, Florida	Mixed Used Development (MXD) Ordinance	Duany Plater-Zyberk with input and approval given by various city departments	http:www.jupiter.fl.us/P&Z/Files/mxd.pdf
Louisville Metro Government, Kentucky	Old Louisville/Limerick Traditional Neighborhood Zoning District Land Development Code including Form Districts	Louisville Metro Staff with Clarion Associates	www.loukymetro.org/Department/PlanDesign/ldc.asp.
1. Miami-Dade County, Florida	Traditional Neighborhood Development Code	Duany Plater-Zyberk and County Staff	http:www.co.miami-dade.fl.us/planzone/
2. Miami-Dade County, Florida	Kendall Downtown Urban Center (KDUC)	Dover-Kohl and Partners, Duany Plater-Zyberk, County Staff	http:www.co.miami-dade.fl.us/planzone/
McKinney, Texas	McKinney Regional Employment Center, Urban Design Standards	Gateway Planning Group and Duany Plater-Zyberk	www.mckinneytexas.org/newurbanism
Monroe, Michigan	TND Ordinance	Urban Design Associates and City Staff	
1. Orlando, Florida	Traditional Neighborhood Development Code	Duany Plater-Zyberk and Coffey and McPherson	www.cityoforlando.net/planning/deptpage/curproj.htm
2. Orlando, Florida	Southeast Orlando Sector Plan Development Guidelines and Standards (Chapter 68 of City Land Development Code)	Calthorpe Associates	www.cityoforlando.net/planning/deptpage; and fws.municode.com

Status as of 5/15/04	Capsule Description	Condition	Area(s) Covered	Application of New Urbanist Regulations
Adopted November 19, 1996	Full New Urbanist code replaced conventional zoning	Infill and urban expansion	Whole jurisdiction	Hybrid
Adopted 1995	Ordinance proposes planned unit developments (PUDs) that incorporate concepts of traditional neighborhood developments (TNDs)	Infill	Whole Jurisdiction	Mandatory
TNZD adopted November 2002; form based code adopted August 2002 for March 2003 implementation	Revised land development code for all localities in Jefferson County creating a two-tier code with zoning and form districts working in tandem. Design, sign, landscape, lighting, and other standards vary by form district.	Full range of conditions	Louisville Metro area	Mandatory
Adopted 1993	Traditional neighborhood development (TND) standards provide a stronger community through architecturally contextual buildings and public spaces, which also contain a mix of uses within a higher-density district.		Agricultural or other low-density residential zoning districts	Optional
Adopted December 1999	The new district replaces existing districts with the goal of producing an urban area with an intensity appropriate for a transit-oriented district, an interconnected street network, good public open spaces in specified locations, and buildings that front on open spaces and streets.	Infill, reuse, and intensification sites	Kendall Downtown and other smaller sites of about 50 to 75 acres near light rail transit stops	Optional
Adopted February 1, 2000	Design standards organized and divided into three overlay zoning categories, completed by a set of standards applicable to the whole area.	Urban expansion	Regional employment center	Mandatory
Adopted 1999	Traditional neighborhood development (TND) adopted as optional zoning district that can be applied to areas currently zoned agricultural or low-density residential, includes pattern book defining architectural styles.	Urban expansion.	Applied at option of developer to greenfield sites	Optional
Not adopted	Full optional New Urbanist code. Creates three regional zoning categories: Rural (to remain undevelopped), Urban (mixed-use), and District (specialized single-use). The Urban category is subdivided in six specific zones ranging in character from urban to rural.	Full range of conditions	Whole jurisdiction. Mapped at request of applicant	Parallel
Adopted October 1999	Regulations implementing New Urbanist plan for major urban expansion area	Greenfield	19,300-acre urban expansion area	Mandatory for most area properties

(Continued on the next page)

Appendix A: Summary Table of New Urbanist Land Development Regulations (cont'd)

PART 3. LOCAL REGULATIONS

Local Government	Title	Prepared By	Electronic Contact
Pasadena, California	Multifamily residential districts (City of Gardens)	Solomon ETC	www.ci.pasadena.ca.us/planning/deptorg/ dhp/gardens.asp
Petaluma, California	Central Petaluma Specific Plan and SmartCode	Fisher and Hall Urban Design with assistance from Crawford Multari and Clark Associates, Sargent Town Planning, and others	http:ci.petaluma.ca.us/cdd/cpsp.html
Saint Paul, Minnesota	Saint Paul Urban Village Code	URS Corp. and City Staff	www.stpaul.gov/depts/ped
San Antonio, Texas	Unified Development Code (Chapter 35)	Freilich, Leitner & Carlisle (Mark White)	http:www.sanantonio.gov/dsd/udc
Sarasota, Florida	SmartCode for Downtown Sarasota	Duany Plater-Zyberk	www.ci.sarasota.fl.us/plan.nsf
Seattle, Washington	Station Area Overlay District Ordinances	City Staff	www.cityofseattle.net/planning/ transportation/SAP/CouncilActions.htm
Skaneateles, New York	Village of Skaneateles Zoning Law	Joel Russell	www.townofskaneateles.com/index.shtml
Sonoma, California	Development Code	Crawford, Multari & Clark and Moule & Polyzoides	www.sonomacity.org/Departments/planning
Suffolk, Virginia	Unified Development Ordinance (some provisions preempted by state statute)	Freilich Leitner & Carlisle	www.suffolk.va.us/citygovt/udo/index.html
Washington County, Oregon	Community Development Code	Planning Staff	www.co.washington.or.us/deptmts/lut/plan01/ codepdf/code.htm
Western Australia	Liveable Neighbourhoods: A Western Australian Government Sustainable Cities Initiative	Western Australian Planning Commission, Ecologically Sustainable Design	www.planning.wa.gov.au/cgi-bin

Status as of 5/15/04	Capsule Description	Condition	Area(s) Covered	Application of New Urbanist Regulations
Adopted February 1989	Regulations specific to multifamily buildings based on detailed study of local building and landscape tradition	Infill	All areas zoned for multifamily use	Mandatory
Adopted June 2003	Form based SmartCode creating three new mixed-use zones based on the rural-to-urban transect.	Infill and reuse	400-acre infill area	Mandatory
Adopted April 2004; in effect May 30, 2004	Three new districts providing for mixed-use areas at different densities and adding design guidance, incorporated in the city's zoning code.	Infill and major reuse sites	Major redevelopment sites	Mandatory
Adopted May 2001	New code for entire City with mandatory and optional provisions both incorporating New Urbanist principles	Full range of conditions	Whole jurisdiction	Hybrid
Public hearings, Spring 2004	Early draft of code for Downtown using Smartcode, proprietary regulatory system developed by Duany Plater Zyberk	Infill	Downtown core, two waterfront districts, and three adjoining neighborhoods	Undecided, likely to be mandatory
Adopted July 2001	Overlay code for future light rail station areas, works in combinaison with underlying station area zoning	Infill	Eight areas surrounding planned rail stations	Mandatory
Adopted 1996	New urbanist regulations for established village center	Infill	Village Downtown	Mandatory
Adopted 2004	New code for the entire city with provisions incorporating New Urbanist principles (e.g., standards and guidelines for streetscape and block structure or mixed-use districts).	Full range of conditions	Whole jurisdiction	Mandatory
Adopted 2000	New code with provisions incorporating New Urbanist principles. It establishes several Use Patterns that set flexible regulations to regulate the form and structure of future development.	Full range of conditions	Whole jurisdiction	Hybrid
Adopted 1997	Regulation establishes nine transit-oriented development (TOD) districts distinguished by differences in emphasis on primary uses and intensity of development. Each of these, however, shares a number of design and development standards. Two overlay districts ensure development compatible with transit in areas surrounding future transit stations.	Full range of conditions	Areas surrounding existing and planned transit stations	Mandatory
Adopted June 1, 2000	State planning strategy allowing developers to choose an alternative to the current policies governing subdivisions and structure plans. It operates as a development code to facilitate the development of sustainable communities.	Greenfield or major infill	Whole jurisdiction. Mapped at request of applicant	Parallel

Charter of the New Urbanism

The Congress for the New Urbanism views disinvestment in central cities, the spread of placeless sprawl, increasing separation by race and income, environmental deterioration, loss of agricultural lands and wilderness, and the erosion of society's built heritage as one interrelated community-building challenge.

We stand for the restoration of existing urban centers and towns within coherent metropolitan regions, the reconfiguration of sprawling suburbs into communities of real neighborhoods and diverse districts, the conservation of natural environments, and the preservation of our built legacy.

We recognize that physical solutions by themselves will not solve social and economic problems, but neither can economic vitality, community stability, and environmental health be sustained without a coherent and supportive physical framework.

We advocate the restructuring of public policy and development practices to support the following principles: neighborhoods should be diverse in use and population; communities should be designed for the pedestrian and transit as well as the car; cities and towns should be shaped by physically defined and universally accessible public spaces and community institutions; urban places should be framed by architecture and landscape design that celebrate local history, climate, ecology, and building practice.

We represent a broad-based citizenry, composed of public and private sector leaders, community activists, and multidisciplinary professionals. We are committed to reestablishing the relationship between the art of building and the making of community, through citizen-based participatory planning and design.

We dedicate ourselves to reclaiming our homes, blocks, streets, parks, neighborhoods, districts, towns, cities, regions, and environment.

We assert the following principles to guide public policy, development practice, urban planning, and design:

The Region: Metropolis, City, and Town

1. Metropolitan regions are finite places with geographic boundaries derived from topography, watersheds, coastlines, farmlands, regional parks, and river basins. The metropolis is made of multiple centers that are cities, towns, and villages, each with its own identifiable center and edges.

2. The metropolitan region is a fundamental economic unit of the contemporary world. Governmental cooperation, public policy, physical planning, and economic strategies must reflect this new reality.

3. The metropolis has a necessary and fragile relationship to its agrarian hinterland and natural landscapes. The relationship is environmental, economic, and cultural. Farmland and nature are as important to the metropolis as the garden is to the house.

4. Development patterns should not blur or eradicate the edges of the metropolis. Infill development within existing urban areas conserves environmental resources, economic investment, and social fabric, while reclaiming marginal and abandoned areas. Metropolitan regions should develop strategies to encourage such infill development over peripheral expansion.

5. Where appropriate, new development contiguous to urban boundaries should be organized as neighborhoods and districts, and be integrated with the existing urban pattern. Noncontiguous development should be organized as towns and villages with their own urban edges, and planned for a jobs/housing balance, not as bedroom suburbs.

6. The development and redevelopment of towns and cities should respect historical patterns, precedents, and boundaries.

7. Cities and towns should bring into proximity a broad spectrum of public and private uses to support a regional economy that benefits people of all incomes. Affordable housing should be distributed throughout the region to match job opportunities and to avoid concentrations of poverty.

8. The physical organization of the region should be supported by a framework of transportation alternatives. Transit, pedestrian, and bicycle systems should maximize access and mobility throughout the region while reducing dependence upon the automobile.

9. Revenues and resources can be shared more cooperatively among the municipalities and centers within regions to avoid destructive competition for tax base and to promote rational coordination of transportation, recreation, public services, housing, and community institutions.

The Neighborhood, the District, and the Corridor

1. The neighborhood, the district, and the corridor are the essential elements of development and redevelopment in the metropolis. They form identifiable areas that encourage citizens to take responsibility for their maintenance and evolution.

2. Neighborhoods should be compact, pedestrian-friendly, and mixed-use. Districts generally emphasize a special single use, and should follow the principles of neighborhood design when possible. Corridors are regional connectors of neighborhoods and districts; they range from boulevards and rail lines to rivers and parkways.

3. Many activities of daily living should occur within walking distance, allowing independence to those who do not drive, especially the elderly and the young. Interconnected networks of streets should be designed to encourage walking, reduce the number and length of automobile trips, and conserve energy.

4. Within neighborhoods, a broad range of housing types and price levels can bring people of diverse ages, races, and incomes into daily interaction, strengthening the personal and civic bonds essential to an authentic community.

5. Transit corridors, when properly planned and coordinated, can help organize metropolitan structure and revitalize urban centers. In contrast, highway corridors should not displace investment from existing centers.

6. Appropriate building densities and land uses should be within walking distance of transit stops, permitting public transit to become a viable alternative to the automobile.

7. Concentrations of civic, institutional, and commercial activity should be embedded in neighborhoods and districts, not isolated in remote, single-use complexes. Schools should be sized and located to enable children to walk or bicycle to them.

8. The economic health and harmonious evolution of neighborhoods, districts, and corridors can be improved through graphic urban design codes that serve as predictable guides for change.

9. A range of parks, from tot-lots and village greens to ballfields and community gardens, should be distributed within neighborhoods. Conservation areas and open lands should be used to define and connect different neighborhoods and districts.

The Block, the Street, and the Building

1. A primary task of all urban architecture and landscape design is the physical definition of streets and public spaces as places of shared use.

2. Individual architectural projects should be seamlessly linked to their surroundings. This issue transcends style.

3. The revitalization of urban places depends on safety and security. The design of streets and buildings should reinforce safe environments, but not at the expense of accessibility and openness.

4. In the contemporary metropolis, development must adequately accommodate automobiles. It should do so in ways that respect the pedestrian and the form of public space.

5. Streets and squares should be safe, comfortable, and interesting to the pedestrian. Properly configured, they encourage walking and enable neighbors to know each other and protect their communities.

6. Architecture and landscape design should grow from local climate, topography, history, and building practice.

7. Civic buildings and public gathering places require important sites to reinforce community identity and the culture of democracy. They deserve distinctive form, because their role is different from that of other buildings and places that constitute the fabric of the city.

8. All buildings should provide their inhabitants with a clear sense of location, weather, and time. Natural methods of heating and cooling can be more resource-efficient than mechanical systems.

9. Preservation and renewal of historic buildings, districts, and landscapes affirm the continuity and evolution of urban society.

Making Great Communities Happen

The American Planning Association provides leadership in the development of vital communities by advocating excellence in community planning, promoting education and citizen empowerment, and providing the tools and support necessary to effect positive change.

472. Converting Storefronts to Housing: An Illustrated Guide. July 1997. 88pp.

473. Subdivision Design in Flood Hazard Areas. Marya Morris. September 1997. 62pp.

474/475. Online Resources for Planners. Sanjay Jeer. November 1997. 126pp.

476. Nonpoint Source Pollution: A Handbook for Local Governments. Sanjay Jeer, Megan Lewis, Stuart Meck, Jon Witten, and Michelle Zimet. December 1997. 127pp.

477. Transportation Demand Management. Erik Ferguson. March 1998. 68pp.

478. Manufactured Housing: Regulation, Design Innovations, and Development Options. Welford Sanders. July 1998. 120pp.

479. The Principles of Smart Development. September 1998. 113pp.

480/481. Modernizing State Planning Statutes: The Growing Smart℠ Working Papers. Volume 2. September 1998. 269pp.

482. Planning and Zoning for Concentrated Animal Feeding Operations. Jim Schwab. December 1998. 44pp.

483/484. Planning for Post-Disaster Recovery and Reconstruction. Jim Schwab, et al. December 1998. 346pp.

485. Traffic Sheds, Rural Highway Capacity, and Growth Management. Lane Kendig with Stephen Tocknell. March 1999. 24pp.

486. Youth Participation in Community Planning. Ramona Mullahey, Yve Susskind, and Barry Checkoway. June 1999. 70pp.

489/490. Aesthetics, Community Character, and the Law. Christopher J. Duerksen and R. Matthew Goebel. December 1999. 154pp.

493. Transportation Impact Fees and Excise Taxes: A Survey of 16 Jurisdictions. Connie Cooper. July 2000. 62pp.

494. Incentive Zoning: Meeting Urban Design and Affordable Housing Objectives. Marya Morris. September 2000. 64pp.

495/496. Everything You Always Wanted To Know About Regulating Sex Businesses. Eric Damian Kelly and Connie Cooper. December 2000. 168pp.

497/498. Parks, Recreation, and Open Spaces: An Agenda for the 21st Century. Alexander Garvin. December 2000. 72pp.

499. Regulating Home-Based Businesses in the Twenty-First Century. Charles Wunder. December 2000. 37pp.

500/501. Lights, Camera, Community Video. Cabot Orton, Keith Spiegel, and Eddie Gale. April 2001. 76pp.

502. Parks and Economic Development. John L. Crompton. November 2001. 74pp.

503/504. Saving Face: How Corporate Franchise Design Can Respect Community Identity (revised edition). Ronald Lee Fleming. February 2002. 118pp.

505. Telecom Hotels: A Planners Guide. Jennifer Evans-Crowley. March 2002. 31pp.

506/507. Old Cities/Green Cities: Communities Transform Unmanaged Land. J. Blaine Bonham, Jr., Gerri Spilka, and Darl Rastorfer. March 2002. 123pp.

508. Performance Guarantees for Government Permit Granting Authorities. Wayne Feiden and Raymond Burby. July 2002. 80pp.

509. Street Vending: A Survey of Ideas and Lessons for Planners. Jennifer Ball. August 2002. 44pp.

510/511. Parking Standards. Edited by Michael Davidson and Fay Dolnick. November 2002. 181pp.

512. Smart Growth Audits. Jerry Weitz and Leora Susan Waldner. November 2002. 56pp.

513/514. Regional Approaches to Affordable Housing. Stuart Meck, Rebecca Retzlaff, and James Schwab. February 2003. 271pp.

515. Planning for Street Connectivity: Getting from Here to There. Susan Handy, Robert G. Paterson, and Kent Butler. May 2003. 95pp.

516. Jobs-Housing Balance. Jerry Weitz. November 2003. 41pp.

517. Community Indicators. Rhonda Phillips. December 2003. 46pp.

518/519. Ecological Riverfront Design. Betsy Otto, Kathleen McCormick, and Michael Leccese. March 2004. 177pp.

520. Urban Containment in the United States. Arthur C. Nelson and Casey J. Dawkins. March 2004. 130pp.

521/522. A Planners Dictionary. Edited by Michael Davidson and Fay Dolnick. April 2004. 460pp.

523/524. Crossroads, Hamlet, Village, Town (revised edition). Randall Arendt. April 2004. 142pp.

525. E-Government. Jennifer Cowley. May 2004. 43pp.

526. Codifying New Urbanism. Congress for the New Urbanism. May 2004. 97pp.